TREKKING THE GIANTS' TRAIL: ALTA VIA 1 THROUGH THE ITALIAN PENNINE ALPS

I0869025

About the Author

Andy, born and bred in Northern England, developed his early mountain skills with his local scout group in the hills of the Lake District and Snowdonia. Since discovering the joys of the Alps with a Cicerone guidebook in 1999, Andy and his wife Sue have explored much of the Western Alps, walking, running, cycling, ski touring or snowshoeing.

Since the late 1980s Andy has enjoyed leading others in the mountains, and he worked as a hillwalking leader before joining the teaching profession. With 25 years' service in Dartmoor Search and Rescue, Andy has vast experience of the moors and recently completed the in-depth training and assessments to become a qualified International Mountain Leader.

When not in school, Andy is likely to be found in the Western Alps, on Dartmoor or in the mountains of Britain.

Other Cicerone guides by the author

Mountain Adventures in the Maurienne

TREKKING THE GIANTS' TRAIL: ALTA VIA 1 THROUGH THE ITALIAN PENNINE ALPS

BENEATH MONT BLANC, THE MATTERHORN AND MONTE ROSA

by Andy Hodges

CICERONE

JUNIPER HOUSE, MURLEY MOSS,
OXENHOLME ROAD, KENDAL, CUMBRIA LA9 7RL
www.cicerone.co.uk

© Andy Hodges 2020
First edition 2020
ISBN: 978 1 85284 992 4

MIX
Paper from responsible sources
FSC® C004791

Printed in Singapore by KHL using responsibly sourced paper.
A catalogue record for this book is available from the British Library.
All photographs are by the author unless otherwise stated.

Route mapping by Lovell Johns www.lovelljohns.com
Contains OpenStreetMap.org data © OpenStreetMap contributors, CC-BY-SA. NASA relief data courtesy of ESRI

To Sue, my partner on every journey, including the longest, our marriage of 26 years. Thank you.

Updates to this Guide

While every effort is made by our authors to ensure the accuracy of guidebooks as they go to print, changes can occur during the lifetime of an edition. Any updates that we know of for this guide will be on the Cicerone website (www.cicerone.co.uk/992/updates), so please check before planning your trip. We also advise that you check information about such things as transport, accommodation and shops locally. Even rights of way can be altered over time.

The route maps in this guide are derived from publicly available data, databases and crowd-sourced data. As such they have not been through the detailed checking procedures that would generally be applied to a published map from an official mapping agency, although we have reviewed them closely in the light of local knowledge as part of the preparation of this guide.

We are always grateful for information about any discrepancies between a guidebook and the facts on the ground, sent by email to updates@cicerone.co.uk or by post to Cicerone, Juniper House, Murley Moss, Oxenholme Road, Kendal, LA9 7RL.

Register your book: to sign up to receive free updates, special offers and GPX files where available, register your book at www.cicerone.co.uk.

Front cover: Approaching Berrio Dessus and the descent to Ollomont (Stage 12)

CONTENTS

Acknowledgements

I would like to thank everyone who has helped to make this project a reality: the wonderful guardians of the refuges and the welcoming hotel owners (particularly Maura at Hotel Valentino and both Monique and Daniela at Etoile du Berger) for making us feel at home; and the Coombe Dean School Exped group for trialling the trek from Valtournenche to Courmayeur.

The team at Cicerone deserve a big thanks: for suggesting the route to begin with; for answering countless questions, providing advice, feedback and editorial direction; and for making this idea a reality.

Thank you most of all to Sue, my wife, for travelling this and every other journey in life at my side. Without you life would be a lonely journey indeed.

Mt Emilius and the Valpelline valley (Stage 12)

Mountain safety

Every mountain walk has its dangers, and those described in this guidebook are no exception. All who walk or climb in the mountains should recognise this and take responsibility for themselves and their companions along the way. The author and publisher have made every effort to ensure that the information contained in this guide was correct when it went to press, but, except for any liability that cannot be excluded by law, they cannot accept responsibility for any loss, injury or inconvenience sustained by any person using this book.

International distress signal *(emergency only)*
Six blasts on a whistle (and flashes with a torch after dark) spaced evenly for one minute, followed by a minute's pause. Repeat until an answer is received. The response is three signals per minute followed by a minute's pause.

Helicopter rescue
The following signals are used to communicate with a helicopter:

Help needed: raise both arms above head to form a 'Y'

Help not needed: raise one arm above head, extend other arm downward

Emergency telephone numbers
Italy: Emergency Services: tel 118

Weather reports
Italy: tel 0165 44 113

Mountain rescue can be very expensive – be adequately insured.

Symbols used on route maps

- route
- alternative route
- start point
- finish point
- start/finish point
- alternative start
- alternative finish
- route direction
- glacier
- woodland
- urban areas
- regional border
- international border
- station/railway
- peak
- manned refuge or hotel/ unmanned refuge
- campsite
- building
- church/monastery/cross
- castle
- pass
- water feature
- viewpoint

Relief
in metres

5000 and above
4800–5000
4600–4800
4400–4600
4200–4400
4000–4200
3800–4000
3600–3800
3400–3600
3200–3400
3000–3200
2800–3000
2600–2800
2400–2600
2200–2400
2000–2200
1800–2000
1600–1800
1400–1600
1200–1400
1000–1200
800–1000
600–800
400–600
200–400
0–200

SCALE: 1:50,000

0 kilometres 0.5 1
0 miles 0.5

Contour lines are drawn at 25m intervals and highlighted at 100m intervals.

GPX files for all routes can be downloaded free at www.cicerone.co.uk/992/GPX.

SWITZERLAND
Western section (Stages 9–16)
Grand Combin
4314m
Chamonix-
Mont-Blanc
Great St Bernard
Monastery
2469m
VAL FERRET
Stage
15b
Stage 15a
Stage 12
Ollomont
Rifugio
Bonatti
Mont Blanc
4810m
VAL DEL GRAN
SAN BERNARDO
Stage 12a
Valpelline
A5
COURMAYEUR
Stage 15
AOSTA
A5
FRANCE
ITALY

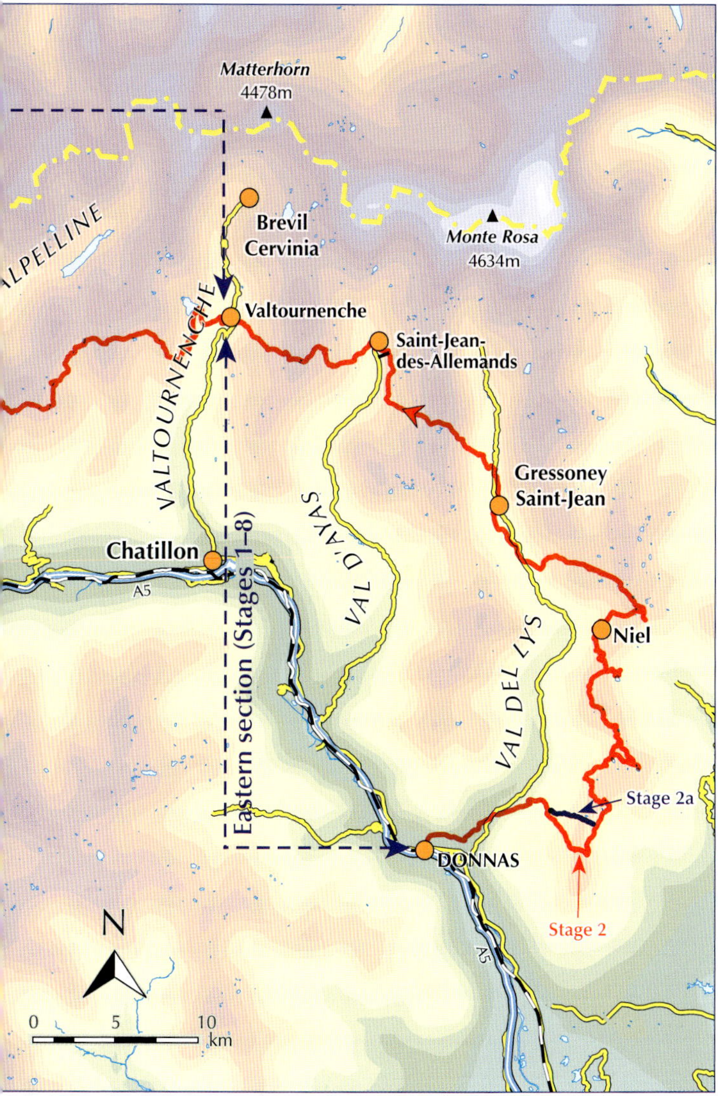
Matterhorn
4478m
Monte Rosa
4634m
Brevil
Cervinia
Valtournenche
Saint-Jean-
des-Allemands
Gressoney
Saint-Jean
Niel
Chatillon
DONNAS
VALPELLINE
VALTOURNENCHE
VAL D'AYAS
VAL DEL LYS
Eastern section (Stages 1–8)
Stage 2a
Stage 2
A5
A5
N
0
5
10
km

ROUTE SUMMARY TABLE

	Stage	Time	Distance	Ascent	Descent	Page
The classic route						
1	Donnas to Sassa (Etoile du Berger)	5hr 20min	9.8km	1550m	500m	48
2	Sassa (Etoile du Berger) to Rifugio Coda	3hr 50min	7.1km	1050m	250m	55
3	Rifugio Coda to Rifugio Barma	4hr 30min	8.1km	530m	700m	65
4	Rifugio Barma to Niel (La Gruba)	7hr 10min	13.7km	900m	1400m	69
5	Niel (La Gruba) to Gressoney-St-Jean	6hr 45min	16.25km	900m	1140m	75
6	Gressoney-St-Jean to Rifugio Vieux Crest	5hr 50min	11.1km	1400m	900m	102
7	Rifugio Vieux Crest to Rifugio Grand Tournalin	4hr	9.5km	1020m	450m	108
8	Rifugio Grand Tournalin to Cretaz, Valtournenche	3hr 30min	7.6km	300m	1300m	112
9	Cretaz, Valtournenche to Rifugio Barmasse	2hr 10min	4.2km	700m	0m	118
10	Rifugio Barmasse to Rifugio Cunéy	7hr 05min	14.2km	1200m	650m	122
11	Rifugio Cunéy to Closé/Oyace/Lexert	6hr 15min	12.25km	450m	1650m	127
12	Closé/Oyace/Lexert to Ollomont/Rey	5hr 25min	11km	1080m	1150m	133
13	Ollomont/Rey to Rifugio Champillon	2hr 40min	4.3km	1040m	0m	144

	Stage	Time	Distance	Ascent	Descent	Page
14	Rifugio Champillon to Saint-Rhémy-en-Bosses	4hr 35min	13.4km	420m	1300m	148
15	Saint-Rhémy-en-Bosses to Rifugio Bonatti	6hr 45min	16.5km	1320m	900m	153
16	Rifugio Bonatti to Courmayeur	3hr 55min	11.2km	150m	950m	174
Totals		**79hr 45min**	**179.2km**	**14,100m**	**13,240m**	
Alternative stages						
2A	The Col Portola Route: Etoile du Berger to Rifugio Coda	2hr 30min	4.3km	720m	50m	61
3A	Rifugio Coda to Rifugio della Vecchia	8hr 45min	15.2km	1350m	1730m	82
4A	Rifugio della Vecchia to Rifugio Rivetti	5hr 40min	10.1km	1200m	850m	90
5A	Rifugio Rivetti to Gressoney-Saint-Jean	5hr 05min	13.75km	370m	1100m	95
12A	Closé/Oyace/Lexert to Ollomont/Rey: the low route	2hr 45min	9.6km	465m	485m	139
15A	Via Francigena from Saint-Rhémy-en-Bosses to Great St Bernard Monastery	2hr 40min	6.1km	780m	0m	161
15B	Great St Bernard Monastery to Rifugio Bonatti	6hr 50min	15.75km	1150m	1510m	167

Crossing the Torrent de Malatrà near Rifugio Bonatti (Stage 16)

INTRODUCTION

The Monte Rosa mountain chain comes into view (Stage 2)

There can be few people who have not heard of at least one of the Alpine giants of Monte Bianco (Mont Blanc), Monte Cervino (the Matterhorn) or Monte Rosa. These giants, along with the slightly less well-known Gran Combin, form the frontier between Italy and Switzerland and have, between them, created many myths, legends and tales of derring-do.

The most famous mountain journeys across the Alps have taken place in the shadows of these giants, and another lies undiscovered, to be enjoyed in a two-week trek between beautiful mountain huts and picturesque mountain villages. The Alta Via 1 (AV1) follows the northern flank of the upper valley for 180km, climbing over 14,000m in the process, and takes the better part of two weeks to walk. These magnificent white giants grace the valley heads and offer stunning backdrops to each day's journey. By the time you reach Courmayeur, they will be old friends and firm favourites.

History echoes with each step; from the views of the Matterhorn, which were instrumental in informing Whymper's first ascent plans, to the Roman temple and road remains in the Great St Bernard Pass, the Aosta Valley has been a centre for Alpine travel since people began travelling through and across the Alps, and it remains so today. Significant Roman remains in Aosta make for an interesting post-script to the adventure.

As well as offering typical Italian hospitality, the region has a unique Savoyard twist. Until a little over 150 years ago the Kingdom of Savoy reigned and reflections of this are abundant to this day. Not least is the bilingual nature of the area; school French will serve the intrepid, independent traveller well.

As an optional diversion to the Great St Bernard Pass, the Canterbury to Rome pilgrim route, the Via Francigena, should be a serious consideration. Here, the stunning monastery and its hospice, which is also home of the world-famous rescue dog, have offered travellers a bed and warm meal for close to a thousand years.

Modern Aosta is still a hub for travellers, and the centre of the town hosts an impressive range of shops and attractions. Of particular interest to the mountain adventurer will be the outlet shops of a number of Italian equipment manufacturers.

Unusually, the Aosta Valley is named after the town and not the river; this further emphasises the importance of the town as the living heart of the valley.

THE ROUTE

Italian trekkers use the term 'Alta Via' in reference to many long distance routes. In the UK, 'Alta Via' often refers to a specific route in the Dolomites. The AV1 is sometimes also referred to as the Tor des Géants, the Tour of the Giants. This is a fitting title as it wends its way in the shadows of the highest mountains in Italy and indeed the whole of the Alps.

To the south of the main valley lies the Gran Paradiso National Park and the AV1's sister walk, the Alta Via 2, covered by Gillian Price in her Cicerone guidebook. This comprises another two weeks of trekking in equally delightful scenery. The two combine to form the Tor des Géants. Also to the south the Colle del Piccolo San Bernardo (Little St Bernard Pass) climbs its way towards France from the valley floor, and although it may be smaller than the grand col – it is by no means small!

With a combination of white, snowy giants as a backdrop and welcoming, green valleys below the AV1, Aosta is a delight. Quiet trails, far-reaching views and blue skies make for a memorable adventure that ends beneath the mighty Mont Blanc; this could be the best kept secret in the Western Alps.

There are many different options for the AV1 trekker to consider; long days can be undertaken by those keen to make the most of every day, while shorter days allow more time to explore the villages and towns en route as well as time to absorb the culture of this fascinating region. Public transport links the side valleys to the main Aosta Valley and on to Turin, allowing the route to be broken into smaller sections. With Valtournenche at the approximate halfway point, the route can be split into two shorter segments if time doesn't allow for the full trek. Buses and the Trek-Bus service allow walkers to access the main valley from here.

The route can be visualised in two sections, each of which has a number of options. The first section is the eastern section, from Donnas to Valtournenche, which will take seven to nine days; the western section from Valtournenche to Courmayeur will also take from seven to nine days.

The route begins with the eastern section, leaving the lower Aosta Valley at Donnas and climbing to explore the mountains centring on the Mont Mars Nature Reserve before descending to Gressoney-Saint-Jean, a charming, small town in the upper Lys Valley. It then climbs out of this valley westwards to cross the tranquil Ayas Valley before heading over to Valtournenche, home to Breuil-Cervinia at the foot of the Matterhorn (or, more correctly, Monte Cervino in Italian). The western section makes its way towards the valley at the head of which is the Colle St Bernardo (St Bernard Pass); it then crosses the route's highest point, not far short of 3000m at the Col de Malatrà, 2925m, to join the Tour du Mont Blanc (TMB) before descending to Courmayeur at the head of the Aosta Valley.

The traditional route is 16 stages in length, although some of these

The high altitude hamlet of Cheneil (Stage 8)

stages are very short and can be merged to create more satisfying days. Alternatives allow the route to be lengthened to include the stunning Great St Bernard Monastery or to enjoy some time to refresh and restock in the villages and towns en route. Appendix A offers an alternative itinerary should you need to fit the entire trek into a fortnight.

An abundance of accommodation allows trekkers to create an itinerary to suit themselves and, other than in the height of summer, bookings can usually be made at short notice. An exception to this is probably Rifugio Bonatti, which hosts the ever-popular TMB. Booking *rifugi* (refuges) one day ahead is highly recommended if not essential, both for peace of mind and out of courtesy to the refuge staff.

Eastern section: eight stages

From the Aosta Valley the route begins with a significant climb up to the high valleys in which it spends most of its time. The mountains of this section are at the very edge of the Alps and experience more than the usual amount of afternoon cloud. With some of the best refuges you will encounter, this makes for a great week-long trek in its own right.

A plethora of options exist in the first few days, allowing for some acclimatisation via short days and long rests if required.

If completing the whole route in one trek it is possible to 'roll through' Valtournenche and climb to Rifugio Barmasse (Stage 9), only another two and half hours or so, thereby saving a day on the itinerary.

The breathtaking view from Rifugio Coda (Stage 2)

The original route of the Alta Via 1 visited the two refuges across the watershed of the Piedmont: the alternative stages described in this guide allow the purist to follow the original line. The Rifugio della Vecchia, nestled close to a high, haunted mountain lake has a certain other-worldliness to it. The Rifugio Rivetti, perched on a spur, is equally atmospheric in the afternoon mist. Following this route, the trekker is likely to have the trail to themselves for much of the day and will experience a more traditional hut life with fewer modcons.

- Stage 1: Donnas to Sassa (Etoile du Berger)
- Stage 2: Sassa (Etoile du Berger) to Rifugio Coda
- Stage 3: Rifugio Coda to Rifugio Barma
- Stage 4: Rifugio Barma to Niel (La Gruba)
- Stage 5: Niel (La Gruba) to Gressoney-Saint-Jean
- Stage 6: Gressoney-Saint-Jean to Rifugio Vieux Crest
- Stage 7: Rifugio Vieux Crest to Rifugio Grand Tournalin
- Stage 8: Rifugio Grand Tournalin to Cretaz, Valtournenche

Alternatives

- Stage 2A: The Col Portola Route: Sassa (Etoile du Berger) to Rifugio Coda
- Stage 3A: Rifugio Coda to Rifugio della Vecchia
- Stage 4A: Rifugio della Vecchia to Rifugio Rivetti
- Stage 5A: Rifugio Rivetti to Gressoney-Saint-Jean

Western section: eight stages

This makes for a fabulous trek in its own right. Departing from below the Matterhorn and finishing beneath Mont Blanc, this trek is one to be savoured. The option to follow the pilgrim route to the Great St Bernard Monastery will be high on many trekkers' lists.

The alternative stages in the western section allow a fascinating diversion to the Great St Bernard Monastery along the Via Francigena, the original pilgrim road to Rome. The first stage is short – barely three hours – which will allow plenty of time to explore the kennels, museum and monastery, whilst the second stage is a full day's walk to reach the Rifugio Bonatti (a shorter option to Rifugio Frassati is also possible and would leave a final day of about 6 hours). To miss the monastery would be to miss an iconic destination of the Alps.

- Stage 9: Cretaz, Valtournenche to Rifugio Barmasse
- Stage 10: Rifugio Barmasse to Rifugio Cunéy
- Stage 11: Rifugio Cunéy to Closé/Oyace/Lexert
- Stage 12: Closé/Oyace/Lexert to Ollomont/Rey
- Stage 13: Ollomont/Rey to Rifugio Champillon
- Stage 14: Rifugio Champillon to Saint-Rhémy-en-Bosses
- Stage 15: Saint-Rhémy-en-Bosses to Rifugio Bonatti
- Stage 16: Rifugio Bonatti to Courmayeur

Alternatives

- Stage 12a: Closé/Oyace/Lexert to Ollomont/Rey: the low route
- Stage 15a: Via Francigena from Saint-Rhémy-en-Bosses to Great St Bernard Monastery
- Stage 15b: Great St Bernard Monastery to Rifugio Bonatti

GEOGRAPHY

The Aosta Valley is much longer than might be expected; from the Piedmont plain the valley continues to climb over 90km and gains over 1000m in altitude to reach Courmayeur and, shortly after, the valleys of Val Ferret and Val Veny beneath Mont Blanc and the modern road tunnel to Chamonix. The numerous valleys splitting off to the north are longer than any found in the British mountains. The valley, and its road leading to the Colle del Gran San Bernardo, is the longest at 34km in length and forms one of the two international borders with Switzerland.

The Northern Aosta valleys

The significant valleys to the north of the main valley are, from east to west:

The Lys Valley: with the main town of Gressoney-Saint-Jean in the upper valley as the focus, there is a whole host of walking and adventure sports to be had here. Climbing and alpinism are also popular, and the ski lift system at Staffal allows access to the snowline even in high summer. Following the AV1, walkers will spend

THE MONT MARS NATURE RESERVE

A mixture of post-glacial geological features and rare wildlife, plants and animals exist in the high mountains above Gressoney-Saint-Jean and the Lys Valley. Above this lies the small (300ha) Mont Mars Nature Reserve. It is important to heed the signs and advice in the area, and, it goes without saying, ensure no pollution or damage is caused while passing through.

up to a week in the mountains above the valley, including time in the Mont Mars Nature Reserve and a night at the brand-new, wonderfully equipped Rifugio Barma.

The Ayas Valley: Champoluc is a ski resort where many British skiers have begun their skiing careers. It remains a popular resort, and the ski infrastructure allows easy access to the high mountains in the summer. The AV1 traverses the higher valley and only drops to Saint Jacques, a small town at the head of the valley, to begin the climb towards Grand Tournalin.

Valtournenche: Breuil-Cervinia lies at the head of the valley and is a well-known ski centre. The Matterhorn sits above the town, often shrouded by mist in the afternoon, and is the undoubted king of the mountains. The AV1 enters and departs this long valley midway along its length, passing through the small town of Valtournenche.

Valpelline: this less well-known valley has a surprising amount of walking on offer. Quiet, majestic and scenic, it is a secret waiting to be discovered. The AV1 spends the better part of three days in the area.

Great St Bernard Pass: one of the most famous valleys and cols in the Alps, if not the world, it has been a major thoroughfare for thousands of years and echoes to the footsteps of pilgrims passing along the Via Francigena to this day. While the AV1 only crosses the valley, a detour to the monastery (see Stages 15A and 15B) will add just a day to the itinerary and allow walkers the unforgettable experience of staying in, and exploring, the most iconic of mountain monasteries.

Val Ferret: shadowed by Mont Blanc, Val Ferret is the final valley encountered by the AV1, which takes a path high above the valley on its final leg to Courmayeur. On a clear day the view of the peaks of the Mont Blanc range are a veritable who's who of mountain first ascents.

GEOLOGY

The complex geology of the Alps is a book in itself; a geologically young range of mountains that are still growing, they offer a fascinating insight into the power of nature.

Minerals are commonly found in the mountains, and crystal hunting was one of the reasons for ascending the high mountains in the past. Geologists believe significant gold fields exist under Monte Rosa, and an abandoned gold mine can be found near the Etoile du Berger, Sassa (Stage 2).

The Alps began to form into a mountain range when the Tethys Sea existed between what is now Africa and Europe. This warm, shallow sea was the perfect environment for the development of deep layers of limestone. The sea began to reduce as the African tectonic plate moved north during the Palaeogene period. Over the course of around 35 million years, long after the mass extinction that ended the dinosaurs' domination, the sea's sediments evolved into layered sedimentary rocks; these folded over and over again on each other, creating nappes. Nappes are layers of rock that have completely folded over rock that was originally above it (and therefore more recently laid), causing geologically confusing profiles where younger rock ends up beneath older rock. These rocks were later subjected to intense heat and pressure forming various metamorphic rocks, including gneiss and schist.

The resultant layering of rock means that the summit rocks of the Matterhorn were originally part of the African Plate, while those lower on the mountain originate from the ancient seabed of the Tethys Sea, with rock from the Eurasian Plate forming the midlayer.

The gradual growth in height of the mountains eventually resulted in a significant mountain range. It is estimated that this growth is continuing at a rate of about 2mm per year, although erosion is also having an impact on this height.

At the end of the last ice age the mountains began to form into the range we see today. It is hard to imagine even the highest peaks being submerged by immense glaciers reaching as far as Lyon in France. Glacial retreat caused enormous amounts of rockfall, and the peaks 'sharpened' into the present shape. Even now, glaciation continues to erode the mountains.

In recent times glacial retreat and advance has caused changes at a human level. Up until the 1200–1300s the high passes were crossable in summer; however, during the last mini ice age the passes became blocked by ice and snow, and people in the Walser region were unable to return to the Upper Valais. The passes remain icebound today, and the Walser valleys maintain a unique character owing much to their Germanic/Swiss origins.

Both Monte Rosa and Mont Blanc owe their colouring and immense bulk to their geology; formed from ultra-tough granite, they resisted glacial erosion and as such are the two highest mountain massifs in the Alps.

The Colle di Saint-Rhémy and a great viewpoint (Stage 15B)

HISTORY

The indigenous tribes living in the valley were subdued by the might of the Roman Empire and, to protect the route through the Alps to Gaul, Augusta Praetoria Salassorum (Aosta), a large Roman military town, was established. Extensive remains can be found in the valley, notably in Aosta and also lower down the valley in Donnas (the beginning of the AV1), where a section of the original Roman road is still evident running alongside the modern road.

Trade and the route from north-western Europe to Rome cemented the valley's role as a major thoroughfare; to this day the valley (and Aosta in particular) has continued to thrive as a trading centre. The Great St Bernard Pass was critical to this success, and the fame of the monastery, along with the formidable nature of the crossing, continued to spread.

Hannibal is thought to have crossed the Alps via the Great St Bernard Pass (although I have made the same claim for the Col de Clapier in *Mountain Adventures in the Maurienne*). To this day the pass he used remains one of the great archaeological mysteries. No evidence has yet been found to substantiate the claims made by the communities living in and around the great Alpine passes. The description put forward by Livy can be read to fit the Great St Bernard Pass, although other accounts suggest that the Little St Bernard Pass is more likely; both would have been known crossing points at the time.

Aosta was an important city of the Duchy of Savoy, second only to the capital cities of Chambery and, later, Turin. The Aosta coat of arms is centred around the Savoyard shield: a red field with a white cross extending to the edges. At its height, around the turn of the 19th century, the duchy spread from Sardinia to the shores of Lac Leman and on to the Jura Alps. Many of the impressive fortresses date from this period, and the House of Savoy was instrumental in the unification of Italy.

Almost inevitably, Napoleon invaded and left his mark in the valley, most notably recorded in the painting *Napoleon Crossing the Alps* by Jacques-Louis David.

In 1861, following protracted diplomatic negotiations, the Kingdom of Italy was founded with the King of Savoy, Vittorio Emanuele II, as its head. His son Umberto became the second king of Italy and was succeeded by Vittorio Emanuele III, who abdicated in 1946 following a vote in favour of Italy becoming a republic. The House of Savoy family was subsequently banished from Italy. This was repealed in 2002, allowing the family to return.

There is still some dispute over who is the 'real' King of Savoy; both the Duke of Aosta, Prince Amedeo, and the Prince of Naples, Vittorio Emanuele, lay claim to the throne, and both have some justification to their claims. This dispute came to a head in 2004 at the wedding banquet of the son of the King of Spain. After the banquet Vittorio Emanuele punched Prince Amedeo twice in the face. First aid was provided by the Queen of Greece, and King Carlos was reported to have been livid!

Modern developments and the autonomous status of the Valle d'Aosta mean the valley is a thriving economy. Since the ski holiday explosion during the 1960s–1970s Courmayeur, Aosta and the valleys have had a new lease of life, and ski holiday infrastructure is evident in many places. Although, in places, this can feel like a despoiled landscape, it is also important to remember that it has created a vast number of jobs and career opportunities for the local population. The 'white gold' of winter holidays has brought wealth and opportunity to what was once little more than a difficult time of year.

ART AND CULTURE

The region has long been independently spirited. As a principal city of the Kingdom of Savoy, Aosta has a strong cultural identity. Artisanal products are celebrated within the town throughout the year and regular cultural events take place during the summer to promote locally made items; the most efficient way to find out what is currently happening is to visit www.lovevda.it.

WALSER CULTURE

The Walser people and their associated cultural identity once spread across the Alps; today small pockets remain in remote corners, with two such areas to be found in the upper Lys valley. Before the mini ice age, which saw rapid glacial advances in the 1300s, people travelled from the Valais to the upper valleys of the Aya and Lys. The passes were ice-free in the summer and so trade and travel were problem-free. Later glacial advances closed off the passes and the people of the Valais who had crossed the mountains found themselves unable to return home.

The distinctive Walser chalet style can be observed in the upper Lys region. The buildings are on stone stilts and have full-width balconies with overhanging upper floors; the balconies often have full-width wooden bars.

The Walser people maintained their own cultural identity, including traditional dress and their language, which bears more than a resemblance to German. Although this has died out to some extent, there is a strong desire to keep the language alive.

Niel – a Walser village high in the Alps and home for the evening at the end of Stage 4

The influence of the church is central to many of the cultural experiences. Every village and most hamlets have well-preserved, ancient churches, chapels or shrines. The adornment and decoration of even the simplest is breathtaking and always worth taking a moment to explore.

Traditional dress is also a feature of village life on festival days, and the trekker may well encounter women and girls dressed in long black dresses with elaborate headwear during Assumption Day celebrations on 15 August. Parades of mountain guides in traditional dress also take place on this day, Courmayeur being particularly notable. It is also common for the local Bureau des Guides to host a celebration of all things mountainous during this week.

PLACES OF INTEREST

You will encounter some small museums and visitor centres along the route that may be of interest. A very small museum in Perloz recognising the partisans of the Second World War is the first, while the museums most likely to be of interest are located in Gressoney-Saint-Jean: the Castel Savoia and Alpenfauna Museum, a regional museum of mountain wildlife. Not far off the route is the Fontina Visitor Centre, between Valpelline and Ollomont, where you can learn all about the local cheese, which is protected under the protected designation of origin scheme. The Great St Bernard Monastery, including its museum and kennels, is also a fascinating visitor attraction should you make the detour. Finally, the destination town of Courmayeur offers the Duke of Abruzzi Alpine Museum in the Société des Guides, which provides a very hands-on experience of old and not-so-old mountaineering.

WILDLIFE

One of the joys of travelling in the mountains is the occasional unexpected encounter with the local wildlife.

The ubiquitous **marmot** will delight the traveller with its antics and panic-stricken whistles at any and every perceived threat. This subterranean, colony-living member of the rodent family is comical in its manner. A shrill whistle will probably be the first encounter for most walkers. A sentry can often be seen on a high outcrop or standing on a grassy knoll while members of the colony feed on the vegetation contentedly. When a predator or other threat is perceived, the whistle will send the grazers scuttling for the cover of their burrows. Two distinct whistles may be heard: one for airborne threats and a different one for ground-based predators.

The majestic **ibex** may be seen surveying his kingdom from rocky outcrops, and you might spot the elegant **chamois** leaping across impossible slopes with ease. These two creatures, vaguely similar to mountain goats in appearance, are less frequently encountered and tend to live in the higher mountains in more secluded spots. You are more likely to come across them off the beaten path, close to the rock–vegetation line, but you might see them close at hand on a remote path.

Eagles and **vultures** soar the skies and are not an infrequent sight. The eagle will keep a close eye on young grazing marmots, while vultures are adept at 'cleaning up' carcasses of both chamois and ibex that have fallen from high mountains or which may have been caught in spring avalanches.

Ibex (French: **bouquetin***) above the Great St Bernard Monastery (Stage 15A)*

In the lower reaches of the route in particular, you will encounter **lizards** of all shapes and colours basking in the summer sun on walls and cliffs.

You will also come across a myriad of **butterflies** along with thousands of **grasshoppers** in the lower fields and pastures.

PLANTS AND FLOWERS

The area covered in this guide offers the walker a vast range of climatic conditions for wildflowers. The lower slopes provide the ideal conditions for growing grapes for wine production, woodlands offer walnuts and hazelnuts galore and the upper mountains allow the keen-eyed walker many opportunities to admire the abundance of wildflowers. Early summer is the optimum time to see the flowers in full bloom; to walk through endless flower meadows is a true delight.

As the altitude increases so the range of flowers changes, with many growing only in the rocky environment of the Alps. A specialist book is recommended, such as Cicerone's *Alpine Flowers* by Gillian Price (author of the AV2 companion guidebook). Another useful identification guide is one of the many available apps that allows the user to identify flowers by colour and month.

Some commonly encountered flowers include the following:

Mountain or Alpine Aster (*Aster alpinus*) looks like a large daisy with

dyed-purple petals and can be found from 1400m to over 3000m.

Great Masterwort (*Astrantia major*) is an architecturally interesting plant commonly found in the lower mountains, up to around 1800m.

Spring Gentian (*Gentiana verna*) is a highly protected deep-blue flower that grows at altitudes of up to 2700m.

Bearded Bellflower (*Campanula barbata*) is quite commonly found along the side of the path from around 1000m to 3000m. The 'furry' flowers and distinctive bell shape help with identification. Both blue and white flowers are commonly found.

Bistort (*Persicaria bistorta*) grows widely across the lower Alpine slopes up to an altitude of 3000m. Traditionally used to treat wounds and cuts, bistort is a member of the dock family.

Arnica (*Arnica montana*), sometimes called Leopard's bane, is both poisonous and a protected species, growing at altitudes of up to around 2800m. Traditionally used as a medicinal herb, it is still used today. It can cause skin irritation on contact.

Golden Rod (*Solidago virgaurea*), also known as woundwort, is a commonly found flowering plant with a long history of medicinal uses. As its alternative name suggests, it was used to treat wounds as well as kidney conditions. It works as an antiseptic, an astringent and a diuretic. Other species of goldenrod have been used for a range of purposes; it was used to make rubber, and the original Model T Ford given to Thomas Edison by Henry Ford had tyres made from goldenrod rubber.

Alpenrose (*Rhododendron ferrugineum*) is such a well-known Alpine bloom that almost every town will have a hotel or restaurant named after it. A sub-species of rhododendron, it blooms early and is often dying away by late July. The higher up the mountain it is found, the later it blooms, so you may find it in full bloom high on the mountainside after encountering dying blooms lower down earlier in the day. It grows at altitudes of up to around 2300m.

Eyebright (*Euphrasia*) was traditionally used (as the name suggests) to treat eye conditions such as conjunctivitis, as well as common ailments such as colds and hay fever. Recent medical testing does not support the traditional herbal remedy claims.

Mountain Houseleek (*Sempervivum alpinum*) is a distinctive-looking plant found at mid to high altitudes, usually in damp spots. In traditional herbal remedies it was used to treat burns, warts, insect bites and stomach disorders.

Martagon Lily (*Lilium martagon*), also known as the Turk's Cap Lily, is a protected species that grows at altitudes of approximately 2000m

Clockwise from top left: Mountain Aster; Wolf's Bane; Great Masterwort; Martagon Lily; Eyebright; Mountain Houseleek; Spring Gentian

to 2400m. Its distinctive shape and height (up to 1m) make it easy to identify.

Wolf's Bane (*Aconitum vulparia*) is a protected species and highly poisonous. It was used to poison wolves and bears in times past. It should not be touched and there have been reports of people becoming ill from inhaling the pollen; admire it from a distance! It enjoys shaded spots high in the mountains at altitudes of up to around 2500m.

Alpine Toadflax (*Linaria alpina*) grows in the higher mountains, usually in gravelly terrain and above the vegetation line. It is likely to be found in small clumps near the higher cols.

Glacial Mouse Ear (*Cerastium alpinum*) is another 'rockery' plant that grows at mid to high altitudes.

Alpine Rose (*Rosa alpina*), not to be confused with Alpenrose, is a wild rose that is usually pink with a yellow-white heart.

Edelweiss (*Leontopodium nivale*), a rare and protected flower, probably epitomises Alpine flowers like no other. Traditionally, it represents devotion or dedication and was a symbol of the resistance to Nazism in Germany. Today it is often used as an emblem in restaurants and as a decoration symbolising the Alps.

As can be imagined, many of these flowers are rare, often enjoying stringent legal protection. Some of these plants are irritants or even harmful to touch. Enjoy them from a distance, take photographs but leave them to grow and prosper in their natural environment.

Other regularly occurring wayside plants of interest include the 'fruits of the forest'; tiny **Alpine strawberries**, as well as **raspberries** and **blackberries**, are often seen growing by the side of paths.

A higher altitude fruit is the **mirtillo** (French: *myrtille*), which is a small, almost black, blueberry. It is common in parts of the UK and is known by a number of names, including whortleberry, bilberry or lingonberry. If 'wayside snacking' is to be enjoyed, it is essential that the fruits are clearly identified, as other berries also grow along the wayside, not all of which are edible.

WEATHER

The first few days of the AV1 take in the very edge of the Alps, and fine views to Piedmont are often to be had in the mornings. As the Italian plain heats up each day, the air rises and meets the cooler air of the mountains, causing considerable cloud formation. It is fairly usual to find the afternoons are cloudy and, if staying at the Coda, Barma, Vecchia or Rivetti refuges, it is likely that you will arrive in mist or fog. The following morning (and possibly the evening before) there will be clear skies and you will be treated to far-reaching views.

The usual Alpine weather cycle is also to be expected, with warm days developing into thunderstorms in the late afternoon. They are not usually a daily event but tend to develop over a few days and then reset. Early starts are always a good plan; to be sitting in a refuge enjoying a coffee and some well-earned cake while hail rattles the windows is far more preferable than a late start and a drenching in a thunderstorm!

Snow can be a problem early in the season, and can also fall overnight by mid-August (although it tends to melt quite quickly in the morning). Old snow can lie about in shaded hollows at higher altitudes even in the height of summer.

Early and late in the season will see a cold start to the day with the possibility of some frost outside the higher refuges. In the middle of summer the temperature can climb to over 30°C in the lower valleys during the middle of the day. A slightly chilly early morning, requiring a light fleece, followed by afternoon temperatures in the mid 20s is more typical in the high mountains during the height of the season. Early and late season trekkers may well find it chillier in the mornings and after sundown.

WHEN TO GO

Aosta is situated at a relatively low altitude but is surrounded by some of the highest mountains in Europe. It has a warm climate but the high mountains, through which the AV1 winds its way, hold snow long into the summer; the early season trekker will be surprised at how much snow is still lying on the ground in June and even early July. The Great St Bernard Pass only opens in June and closes again in September. The road tunnel maintains year-round vehicular access.

Crossing the long-lasting snow patches close to Rifugio Cunéy (Stage 10)

Most mountain refuges are only open from late June until early to mid September; to complete the trek outside the high summer season will mean backpacking and will require a high level of mountain skills to cope with late or early season snow and its associated difficulties. The Italian holiday season is from early August until shortly after 15 August (Assumption Day), which is a national holiday (as it is in France and Switzerland too).

Early in the summer the valleys and alpages are carpeted with wildflowers and are a sight to behold. Snow may be lying on the higher ground and each day brings summer a little closer. Late August and early September are also wonderful times; the crowds have dissipated, there is a nip in the air and the first hints of autumn are visible. Wild fruit and nuts can be foraged, the refuges are still open and the valley hotels are no longer charging high-season prices.

ACCESS AND TRAVEL

It is feasible to travel from the UK and arrive in the valley by late afternoon if travelling by air, and within two days if driving. With modern, fast trains, travelling by rail is another realistic option.

By air

Turin is the nearest airport and it is a comparatively easy onward journey to the Aosta Valley. Regular train and bus routes operate from Turin, most of which change in Ivrea. Trains to Aosta (and stations lower in the valley, particularly Donnas) are regular – approximately every hour each day.

It is also fairly straightforward to fly to Geneva and then continue to the valley via the Mont Blanc Tunnel. A number of private transfer companies operate a service at a reasonable cost.

By car

The journey from UK ports to the Aosta Valley can be a treat in itself. The famous towns of Reims and Troyes are worthy stopover points. The journey from there is either via Besançon and then Switzerland and over the mighty Great St Bernard Pass or via Chamonix and the Mont Blanc Tunnel; both have merits and offer different views and opportunities en route. The difficulties of leaving a car in the valley can be overcome by making arrangements with a hotel in Courmayeur, staying there on the first evening and again on completion of the route. This may be more difficult in the high season (the first half of August in particular). There is a large, free car park in the middle of Aosta that serves the Pila ski lift; to leave a car here is not without risks but the author has left a car there for a week at a time. For those considering only part of the route it is also possible to leave a car free of charge near the Great St Bernard Monastery and take a bus to the main valley.

The tunnels through the Great St Bernard Pass and Mont Blanc are quite expensive (50CHF and €45 return, respectively, in 2018). The road over the Great St Bernard Pass is open during the summer and adds approximately 30min to the journey, as well as the option to visit the monastery.

By train

From the UK it is feasible to travel to Turin by Eurostar, changing to the TGV service in Paris. The journey times can be remarkably quick and are a real alternative to flying. From Turin regular trains travel into the Aosta Valley, usually changing in Ivrea.

IN-ROUTE TRANSPORT OPTIONS

The route, while linear, allows some options to use public transport, although these are limited as the AV1 'crosses the grain' as it makes its way west, which will result in a detour to the main valley to seek transport back up the next valley; these journeys will take up much of the day in many cases.

Some support is available in the eastern valleys in the form of Trek-Bus, which offers very reasonably priced links within the Gressoney, Ayas and Valtournenche valleys. The company will also transfer baggage from and within valleys. To book call + 39 348 4458175 (French and Italian spoken; if needs be, ask a local to help you book). The Trek-Bus service runs in the early morning and late afternoon and must be booked at least the day before.

Regular bus services also serve the valleys. Although these tend to be infrequent and time-consuming, they do operate at important trekking

Alpenzu, a traditional Walser village sitting high above Gressoney-Saint-Jean and the Lys Valley (Stage 6)

times, namely early and later in the day. For example, the Bionaz to Aosta bus departs around 0845 and the next one is around 1500. Savda and SVAP operate bus routes in the valleys. Prices are very reasonable and compare favourably with UK prices.

Information about the bus services can be found at www.svap.it and www.savda.it. It appears that new timetables are produced only when there is a timetable change, hence the most recent timetable may be dated 2016 or even earlier.

A couple of stages can be 'hopped' by bus: from Closé to Ollomont can be managed by bus via Valpelline, and you can also use a bus for the Great St Bernard Monastery (situated at the top of the pass) from Saint-Rhémy-en-Bosses.

Private taxis may be a viable alternative for groups. They are much more expensive than the buses but will allow travellers greater flexibility in travelling and can reduce the transfer time considerably. From Aosta to Saint-Rhémy-en-Bosses will cost around €50, while a bus will be about €4–6.

Appendix B provides contact details of transport providers in the valley.

ACCOMMODATION

The Aosta Valley has a long history of catering for travellers' needs, and there is no shortage of options along the length of the valley as well as in the northern valleys of this guide.

Hotels and a range of B&B options exist in most villages in the valleys and can be researched easily online; alternatively, see www.aosta-valley.co.uk for links to accommodation throughout the area.

While you are trekking the AV1, mountain refuges will be an essential stopover providing a basic but welcoming night's sleep and traditional food in very good locations in the heart of the mountains.

Appendix B lists accommodation for the end of each stage; these details were correct in 2019 but are likely to change over time. Other accommodation is available along the route. Some is still under construction, and signs along the paths indicate *dortoirs* and private refuges that are being constructed or converted.

To complete the AV1 as a backpacking expedition is feasible but not simple; it is usually possible to camp at refuges with the guardian's permission for a small fee. Limited camping options are available in some villages on the route, but this is much less common than in other countries. Wild camping above 2500m is permitted; however, camping below this altitude breaches local laws and regulations (much of the trail is below 2500m). Additionally, fuel for stoves can be hard to come by. One or two shops in Donnas are Camping Gaz stockists but may close in mid to late August for their own holidays. Petrol can be purchased from service stations but usually only as a minimum of 5 litres. And of course, this carries a weight penalty for campers.

MOUNTAIN HUTS

The tradition of mountain huts (Italian: *rifugio*; plural, *rifugi*) is long established and when mixed with the Italian love of quality local food and drink make for a highlight of the journey.

Some of the refuges are owned by the Italian Alpine Club (CAI); these are more likely to have been established 60 or more years ago and tend to cater for walkers and climbers of the higher peaks. They can be perched in spectacular positions, often on the higher slopes of a mountain or on a shoulder protecting it from winter avalanches. All supplies are either carried or, more usually, flown in by helicopter; this means the range is limited and prices tend to be higher for heavier items, as it is linked to the payload of the helicopter.

The CAI honours the reciprocal rights agreement with other Alpine clubs, which charges members of other clubs the same price as CAI members, providing a discount on the dormitory aspect of their stay.

Members of the British Mountaineering Council (BMC) or Alpine Club can apply for a Reciprocal Rights Card, which enables members to access this reduced price. Another alternative is to join the British section of the Austrian Alpine

The bright interior of Rifugio Rivetti (Stage 4A)

Club (AAC), which then permits access to the reciprocal rights agreement. Reciprocal rights discounts are rarely offered in private refuges. The cost of either joining the AAC or purchasing a BMC Reciprocal Rights Card will be recouped after about five nights' use of the CAI refuges.

Most of the refuges on the AV1 are privately owned. These tend to be of a higher standard and are more recently established, often by farming families in the area. As such, they are more accessible by vehicle and therefore have more access to fresh produce and supplies.

Accommodation is usually in dormitories or smaller rooms. A sheet sleeping bag is all you require; all other bedding is provided. Meals are a set affair and are communally served. The hut team will do their best to accommodate dietary requirements but really appreciate advance notice. Vegetarians can often be offered fried eggs or an omelette in lieu of the meat element of the dish, although we enjoyed one of the best vegetable lasagnes ever offered in a refuge at Rifugio Rivetti. Most refuges offer shower facilities, but these can be a bit hit and miss as the electricity is usually solar and will be timed to last only a few minutes.

The private refuges tend to be better served by vehicle tracks or located in summer alpages and therefore have better facilities. Meals may be more of a restaurant style, offering menu choices and private tables. Rooms may also be private and might even be en suite; some can even be described as 'mountain hotels', combining the best aspects of refuges – location and an understanding of mountain travellers' needs – with the higher standards of a hotel, and often at a minimal cost difference.

It is easy to contact the refuges during the season; however, in the off season emails may go unanswered for some time. Some refuges have a social media presence, which may also be worth using as a means of contact.

Hut etiquette

In high summer prior booking is highly recommended, either via email in advance or by phone a day or so ahead. Should your plans change, it is also expected that the booking will be cancelled, otherwise the guardian may well refuse other bookings, waste time contacting other refuges or even initiate an expensive search and rescue as they anxiously await your arrival. A certain code of conduct is expected of hut users in the Alps. Most 'rules' are fairly common sense but failure to adhere to them will earn the miscreant a quick rebuke from the guardian and other users.

On arrival at a hut it is expected that trekking poles are left outside or hung up on pegs. Boots are stored in the entrance area where 'hut slippers' are stored, increasingly these are Crocs in a range of sizes and colours.

The next task is to inform the guardian of your arrival and register;

A gentle start to the day on Stage 10; good tracks head towards the path to Finestra d'Ersa

guardians may request a formal document, such as a passport. The guardian will usually ask where you are travelling on to and may offer a suitable breakfast time, taking this information into account.

You will usually then be shown to your dormitory where a bed may be designated. Spreading your sheet sleeping bag on your bed is a good idea to indicate it is taken. A basket or cubby hole to store personal items is commonly available as well as a shelf near the head of the bed/bunk. It is sensible to keep a headtorch at hand; lighting is often limited and weak as it is generated using solar energy. Damp items can be placed in the drying room or spread out in the sun (once the sun sets the temperature will drop quickly and overnight frost is not unheard of).

A running tab will be kept for additional drinks and snacks and settling up usually takes place after dinner if an early start is planned or after breakfast if not. It is expected that payment will be made in cash in huts. Some of the lower 'mountain hotels' may take a credit card, but this will be the exception rather than the rule.

As everything is flown in and out, it is also expected that any personal rubbish will be taken with you. Waste is increasingly recycled; bottles and packaging bought at the refuge can be left in the recycling bins.

CLOTHING

Hut-to-hut trekking does not require an extensive wardrobe, nor does it require expensive additional equipment beyond that normally used to walk in the UK.

Everything should fit into a 30 to 35 litre rucksack with room to spare for snacks and the odd trinket or two.

Regular trekkers will see many European travellers favouring a poncho over full waterproofs. This is a debatable point; a poncho is cheap, often less than €30, and packs up to quite a small package. It allows more ventilation and most have a 'hunch' to accommodate a backpack. On the downside it does not provide full cover and will flap about a lot in high winds.

Appendix D provides a recommended kit list and advice on the appropriate equipment for an Alpine trek.

FOOD AND DRINK

Water can often be accessed from water pipes in farms and alpages and from public fountains in villages; the author usually takes water from these sources with no ill effect. Tap water from refuges is usually drinkable, but a sign may indicate the water is not drinkable, in which case treatment or buying bottled water is the sensible option.

Packed lunches are available from refuges; they are usually comprehensive and consist of two rolls, some biscuits or cakes, some fruit and maybe one or two other snacks. They tend to be expensive at around €10 per person. Stocking up in village shops can cut down costs, and shops often sell 'long-life' bread that may not be as tasty as freshly baked loaves but it will survive a few days in a pack. Cheese triangles are often sold in shops and do not need to be kept chilled so are fairly trek-proof; a small plastic box for fruit and other consumables is a very useful item to include in your rucksack.

Food production is admired and celebrated in every valley; a range of local produce is usually available and is worth tasting. Great pride is taken in local cheeses and dried meat sausages, all widely available and perfect for lunch packs. A common offer is *taglieri*, a cheese or meat platter, while polenta cooked with local cheese is another regularly encountered delicacy.

Local drinks include a range of beers, wines and fruit-based drinks, but the one most often encountered is *grappa*, a strong spirit made from grapes; as it uses the skin, seeds and pulp of grapes as its base constituents, it is not too difficult to see how it is a by-product of the wine industry.

A wooden container called a *grolla* is often seen in many shops and restaurants. It is a multi-spouted drinking container that is passed around the table after dinner. It contains 'coffee of friendship' (*café de l'amitié*), a strong black coffee in which strong spirits are blended, often *genepi*. The *grolla* is believed to have begun life as a wooden clog shared between shepherds.

LANGUAGE

As would be expected, the first language of the region is Italian but, given the Savoyard roots of the region, French is also widely spoken. English is less likely to be encountered in the mountains, although the main valley settlements often have staff who are able to speak English.

An attempt to speak Italian or French is warmly received and even the most basic attempts will be encouraged and appreciated. A glossary of useful terms and phrases in both Italian and French can be found in Appendix C.

MAPS AND NAVIGATION

Italian cartography varies greatly, and it is rarely up to the standard of Ordnance Survey, IGN in France or Swiss mapping. Some maps have inaccuracies and are of limited use for fine navigation; however, the 1:25,000 Carta dei Sentieri by L'Escursionista editore are of a good standard and are recommended by some of the guide associations in the valleys. Contours are at 25m intervals and there is GPS compatibility. Five maps are needed for the AV1. The most recent versions are printed on a waterproof material, which will be used for all newly produced maps by 2020. They cost around €10 each and are sold in numerous shops in the valleys, but usually the range is limited to the valley you are visiting. Shops in Aosta tend to sell maps for

Reflections on the unnamed lake near the refuge on Stage 10

USEFUL APPS AND RESOURCES

In addition, some phone apps can be a useful supplement to the information within this guidebook:

- **Mapping:** the majority of the route, from Gressoney onwards, can be accessed on Swiss mapping, a free online service is available at www.swisstopo.ch.
- **Weather:** 'Yr.no' is a commonly used and reliable weather app (a Norwegian website provided by the national meteorological and broadcasting services).
- **Alpine flowers:** 'The World of Alpine Flowersie' is an unusually titled but detailed app that allows the user to identify wildflowers by colour and month of the year.

A phrasebook app is also a useful addition; if it is in French as well as Italian, so much the better.

the entire valley. They are also available to purchase online with international postage from www.escursionista.it.

The other option is the 1:50,000 maps by Instituto Geografico Centrale. These maps are of limited use, as the AV1 is not always marked accurately, contours are at 50m intervals meaning much detail is lost and there is no GPS compatibility. Three maps are needed to cover the route.

1:25,000 Carta dei Sentieri by L'Escursionista editore (in order of use)

- 12: Basse Valli d'Ayas e del Lys
- 08: Alte Valli d'Ayas e de Lys, Monte Rosa
- 06: Valpelline St Barthélemy
- 05: Gran San Bernardo, Valle di Ollomont
- 01: Monte Bianco, Courmayeur

1:50,000 maps by Instituto Geografico Centrale (in order of use)

- 9: Ivrea, Biella, Bassa Valle d'Aosta
- 5: Cervino Matterhorn e Monte Rosa
- 4: Massiccio del Monte Bianco

Other maps are available locally at a range of scales. Some are better than others but the 1:25,000 maps from L'Escursionista editore are the best the author has used. As the route is close to the Swiss border much of the route benefits from Swiss maps 'overlapping', so this is a further possibility, although Swiss maps tend to be much more expensive.

WAYMARKING

It is almost universal to use red and white flashes to mark paths in the

Western Alps and this system is continued in Piedmont. However, the vast majority of the AV1 route is in the autonomous region of the Valle d'Aoste. The forestry commission in Aosta uses red and white flashes to mark various areas and therefore paths in the Valle d'Aoste are marked with yellow flashes.

The AV1 is marked by a yellow triangle with a 1 inside and also by yellow arrows. The waymarking is usually clear but can be hidden by foliage in the height of summer and, unfortunately, yellow doesn't stand out as clearly as red and white. Should you decide to descend to the Vecchia or Rivetti refuges, the paths are marked with red and white flashes (that said, the paths to the refuges are obvious without additional marking).

Most path junctions have arrow markers indicating the destination of the path, its altitude and the time expected to walk there. Not as common in the Alps is the Italian practice of numbering paths (1,2,3, etc.) and adding a sub-division (A,B,C, etc.). These are replicated on some maps (particularly those produced locally by tourist information offices). The timings are generally accurate but occasionally there can be discrepancies in both timings and altitudes. There may also be minor variations in spelling and whether 'de, del, della' are included or not.

Other navigational pointers include the signs for popular running events in the valleys and the barely comprehensible Tor des Géants: a 330km race that pretty much follows the AV1 and AV2; the route generally follows the AV1 but deviates at times. The race compresses the AV1 and AV2 into a one-week event for ultra-runners; to walk this route will take over a month, to run it in a week is a challenge beyond most people's imagination. The winners complete it in an unimaginable 70 hours or less!

Waymarking on the AV1; occasional discrepancies in signage can arise!

SAFETY AND EMERGENCIES

The universal European Emergency number (112) can be used to contact the local emergency services. Do not expect the call handler to be able to speak English, although this may well be the case. Be prepared to speak basic Italian or French; composing a phrase or two on paper before making the call may well help. Make sure you can explain where you are and what has happened. Most, but not all, rescues and recoveries will be by helicopter and, therefore, adequate insurance is essential. Make sure any policy covers helicopter evacuation.

A hut guardian will be expecting your arrival and will probably have asked, at the time of booking, from which direction you will be arriving. Giving the guardian your contact details when making the booking (via email or over the phone) is a sensible idea, as they are likely to call you in the event of your non-arrival and will co-ordinate and communicate with rescue services if need be. Should you choose not to use your booking, it is essential that you inform the guardian of your change of plan to avoid unnecessary rescue communications.

In an emergency situation:

- Keep out of the weather – some sort of survival bag, or preferably a bothy bag, will make life substantially more comfortable while waiting for help to arrive
- Keep everyone warm – use spare clothes, huddle together in the bothy bag, put on a hat and gloves early (before the heat has been lost)
- Insulate yourself from the ground – use a small mat or spare equipment to keep off the cold ground
- Make yourselves visible – torches, bright clothing and a suitably visible position will help the rescuers locate the group
- Keep your mobile phone on and free from other traffic – the emergency services may want to

SHEPHERD DOGS

There are often warnings about Patou dogs at work in the area; these are large white shepherding dogs used to protect flocks from wolves and other predators. Should you encounter these dogs:

- stop, preferably together as a group;
- be calm and quiet and allow the dogs to assess you;
- do not shout, run or wave sticks or maps at them as you won't frighten them off;
- if you have a dog, keep it on a lead and close by;
- when the dogs (there are usually two) have lost interest in you, walk calmly and quietly past the flock.

Monte Rosa emerging from cloud on the path to Mont Roux (Stage 2)

call you back. Ensuring adequate phone battery life is also essential; turn off non-essential apps and other power-consuming aspects of your phone.

INSURANCE

To travel in the mountains of Europe without insurance cover is inviting disaster. The European Health Insurance Card (EHIC) is a free card that provides the bearer with basic health care – but it is not an insurance policy. (It is important to note that there may be changes to this agreement post-Brexit.) Many insurance providers expect clients to have an EHIC.

The insurance policy must cover the activities being undertaken; a growing number of insurance providers now offer cover for mountain and adventure sports. The BMC offers a comprehensive scheme for members, which is particularly competitive for those with pre-existing medical conditions and for older trekkers (basic membership of the BMC is a requirement). The AAC provides some cover as part of its basic membership package (be aware that this is not a comprehensive policy and does not cover travel to and from the mountains). Snowcard offers a customisable policy and provides a discount for second members at the same address. Endsleigh offers very good options, including cover for groups. Its policies can also be customised to cover other activities beyond trekking; it is important to ensure that the higher altitude option is included (to cover altitudes of up to 3000m).

Annual policies often offer considerable savings if planning more than two trips abroad.

Helicopter rescue

Helicopters are the most commonly used method of evacuating a casualty from the mountains and will be used in most cases. For this reason, in particular, it is important to ensure your insurance policy covers helicopter evacuation.

USING THIS GUIDE

The AV1 can be tackled in one long walk, which allows plenty of time to relax and unwind, or, for those with less time available, the route can be split into two one-week walks, with Valtournenche making a perfect midway pause. Good local transport allows simple access into and out of Valtournenche from the main Aosta Valley. Options for tackling the AV1 in a variety of formats are included in Appendix A.

An outline of data for each stage of the walk is provided, including average timings, approximate distances and height gain and loss. Height lost can be almost as tiring as that gained and deserves respect and consideration. Some stages have alternatives that allow trekkers to personalise their route in consideration of the weather and fitness of the group. A particularly intriguing option for many will be to divert to the monastery at the Great St Bernard Pass.

At the end of most stages only one accommodation option is available, a mountain hut. On some stages the route ends in a small town or village where a number of options may exist. The contact details of all refuges were up to date in 2019.

Naturally, in a mountain environment paths are subject to erosion and as the winter departs there is often some avalanche damage to paths and river crossings. The guardians of the refuges will be able to offer advice on last-minute route changes, but heavy rainfall can make even simple 'plank bridge' crossings quite challenging; trekking poles are invaluable for providing support.

Timings

Trying to estimate times is always a challenge; the times given in this guidebook are, generally, those indicated on the signposts with real life experience tempering them on occasions. The author tends to walk slower downhill than the signpost times suggest (saving achy knees to some extent) but walks marginally quicker uphill.

As trekkers become fitter, more acclimatised and more familiar with the terrain, they can begin to move quicker than the 'standard' time given on signposts. Sometimes, local Alpine clubs will cover the original times with small wooden panels showing new times (see photo in 'Waymarking'), which demonstrates that they are open to variation and interpretation.

Grading

Route grading is subjective and, as such, difficult to measure for every walker. The trek follows reasonably frequented paths and although the surface is uneven and rocky in places, it is not too challenging. Any section that features more exposure than might be expected will have some fixed ropes as handrails. (In a couple of places the maps denote 'via ferrata' but this falls very much in the realm of an occasional metal foot plate placed on a small rocky lump; fear not, this is not the Dolomites!)

In this guidebook the grading for each stage is as follows:

- **Grade 1:** a simple path with a moderate gradient, suitable for all walkers
- **Grade 2:** a reasonably strenuous Alpine walk, typical of a day in the mountains but not particularly challenging. Usually 5–7 hours in duration
- **Grade 3:** some technical sections where previous Alpine experience will be advantageous. Grade 3 may also be used for particularly long days (over eight hours) that will be physically demanding, mostly with limited acclimatisation.

These match the CAI and local Valle d'Aosta councils' grades. Their denotations are as below:

- **T:** tourist path – a very well-marked, gentle path, usually limited to the valley bottom
- **E:** trekking path – the usual features of a mountain path will be

Looking down the valley, having passed Kiersee lake (Stage 4 and Stage 3A)

The very fine 'Two Monts' ridge (Stage 2)

present without technical difficulties or challenges. Most of the AV1 follows such paths

- **EE:** expert hikers – steep or exposed paths may be encountered, and the ground may be more technical. Sections may be protected with fixed rope handrails and the occasional footstep attached to rock outcrops. Steep rocky sections of path may be encountered for short distances. (Rough Lakeland or Welsh paths would be similar, below Grade 1 scrambling in the UK.)

GPX tracks

GPX tracks for the routes in this guidebook are available to download free at www.cicerone.co.uk/992/GPX. A GPS device is an excellent aid to navigation, but you should also carry a map and compass and know how to use them.

THE ALTA VIA 1: AN ITALIAN HAUTE ROUTE

Approaching Berrio Dessus and the final descent to Ollomont (Stage 12)

EASTERN SECTION

STAGE 1

Donnas to Sassa (Etoile du Berger)

Start	Donnas, railway station
Distance	9.8km
Total ascent	1550m
Total descent	500m
Grade	2
Time	5hr 20min
Maps	1:50,000 Instituto Geografico Centrale 9: Ivrea, Biella, Bassa Valle d'Aosta; 1:25,000 Carta dei Sentieri by L'Escursionista editore 12: Basse Valli d'Ayas e del Lys

The AV1 begins in Donnas at a low height of 330m and encompasses a significant climb of approximately 1500m ascent towards the end of the walk, which finishes at the delightful Etoile du Berger. This will be a tough first day of over five hours' walking that is uphill for pretty much the whole day. There is an alternative, though: the AV1 route crosses the main Lys valley road at the hamlet of Tour d'Hereraz. From here the walk to the Etoile du Berger is approximately three hours and makes for a gentler starting day and also allows those arriving mid morning to begin the trek. It is also possible to link this shorter first day with the shorter option for Day 2, to arrive at Rifugio Coda in about six hours from Remondin, thereby saving a day should time be a pressing issue.

From the railway station in Donnas begin by crossing the road, turning right and walking for about 50 metres. The yellow signpost is visible just after St Pietro in Vincoli, a yellow-painted church. Follow the Via Rue Janin directly uphill, passing a school on the right. The route climbs quite directly through the narrow streets

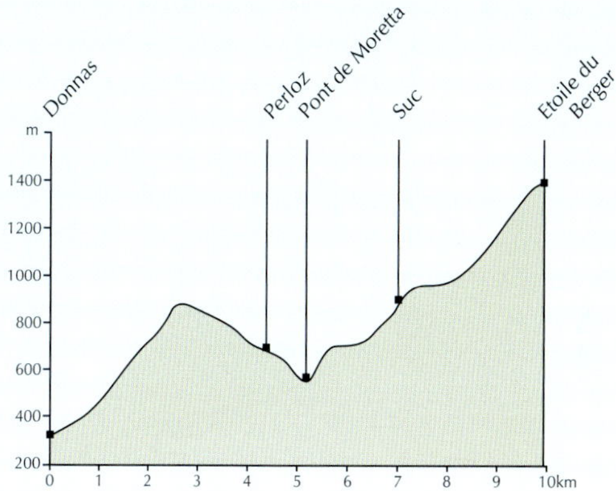

with clear yellow signage aiding route-finding. Narrowed cobbled streets soon give way to a tarmac road and an older track that climbs directly up the hillside. ▸ You will again encounter the tarmac road as this more-direct path cuts the corners by climbing straight upwards. A couple of minutes later climb some stone steps and pass through the unusual gateway at Côte d'Artada, one of a number of shrines en route. Join the tarmac road for about 50 metres to the beautiful church of Sposalizio de Vergine on a hairpin bend. The view above the Aosta Valley already indicates how much height has been gained.

It is easy to imagine the track dating back to Roman times as it wends its way through vineyards.

After the church take a track on the right and almost immediately leave this to take a steeper path on the left. This path climbs the wooded slopes for about 1km. ▸ Pass another shrine and shortly after, join a forest road at approximately 800m altitude. **1hr 20min**

The forest provides welcome shade in the summer months. Later in the season you may see early chestnuts on the ground in their distinctive spiky cases.

Follow this track for a few minutes until just after a sign for 'Place 815m' ('Place de la' on the map). Descend into the woods on a path indicating 'Perloz: 55min'.

As the path descends past a number of small caves, it is not hard to imagine what good hideouts these would have been for Italian partisans from 1943 to

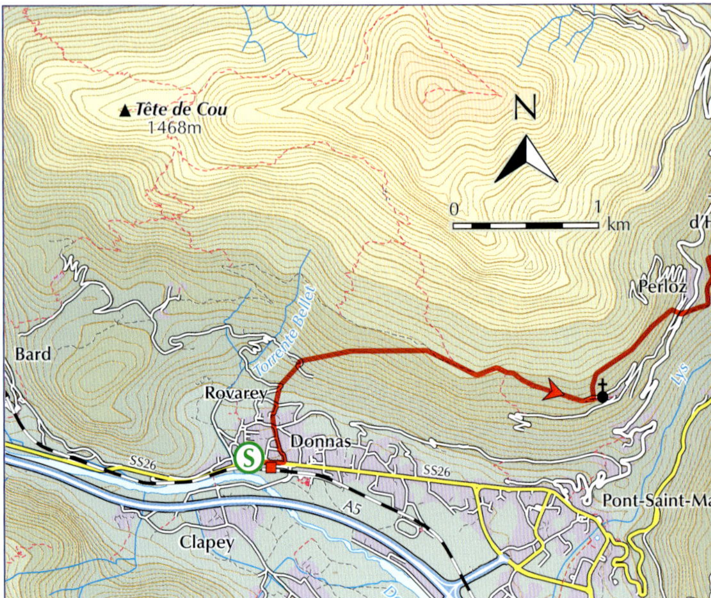

1945; this area was a heartland of the **resistance**, and the small museum at Perloz sheds light on the heroic actions of the local resistance movement during the Nazi occupation in the latter part of the Second World War.

After 20min leave the shade of the woods at the end of the dirt road. You can follow this road instead of taking the signed AV1 path below it. To do so will mean missing out on a visit to the church of Santuario di Notre-Dame-de-la-Garde, which is a beautiful collection of buildings set in a stunning location. **1hr 45min**

Descend to a signpost and just before the church re-ascend to join the dirt track mentioned above, which has, by this time, become a metalled road. The AV1, which is signed left almost immediately, begins a climb of a little over 100m.

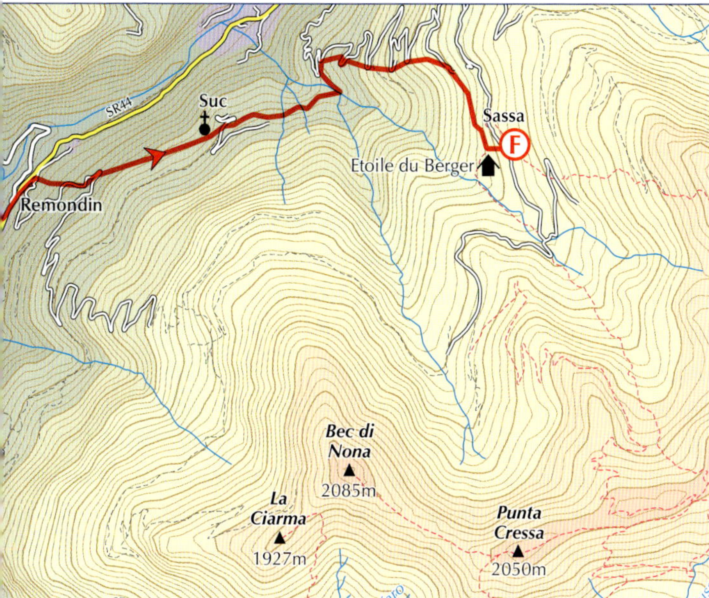

Alternative route to Perloz via the church

Alternatively, you can reach Perloz by continuing to the church and passing it to the right. Take the paved track leading downhill and pass the old village laundry sinks to gain a little-used metalled road, which will take you into Perloz in approximately 15min. You can pick up the AV1 shortly after the Mairie.

After 30min you will reach the high point of 820m. Pass a ruined building and cross a narrow section, which is protected with handrail cables. A short ladder helps with a steep descent and before long the route passes a 'pond'. ▸ Enter **Perloz** via a man-made water channel and pass the TV/mobile phone mast.

The pond appears to be the water supply for Perloz so should be treated with care and respect.

Descend through the village on lovely cobbled streets, too old and narrow for vehicles, to come out opposite the Mairie and the small Musée de la Résistance.

The short, exposed section above Perloz

Carry on through Perloz towards the Pont de Moretta. **2hr 45min**

> The **Pont de Moretta** is a truly impressive piece of construction and, as befits deep gorges and bridges in the Alps, there is a legend to accompany the crossing. This one includes a dragon that burned the previous wooden structure, which is why this one is constructed from stone. An information panel demonstrates the construction techniques used to build the bridge in 1721.

Continue uphill, following the obvious track to the hamlet of **Tour d'Hereraz** and the main road to Gressoney-Saint-Jean. As you arrive in the hamlet, the path joins a tarmacked track climbing leftwards.

The **tower** from which the hamlet takes its name is the church clock tower. Dating back approximately 1000 years, and once part of a fortified structure belonging to the wealthy and powerful Herens family from Valais (modern day Switzerland), it was converted into a church clock tower in 1878 and is one of the oldest structures in the valley.

The road curves to the right. Take a left turn onto a minor road before shortly turning rightwards and climbing a set of steps between two houses. Turn left to join the main road for a couple of hundred metres. **2hr 55min** ▸

If you have used the bus or Trek-Bus option, the route begins here.

Cross the main road and take the minor road to Remondin and Barmette. After you have passed through Barmette and entered the 'centre' of Remondin (a very small hamlet), AV1 signs indicate a right turn onto an ancient mule track; take this track. Before long the route eases its gradient and climbs diagonally across the ancient fields, still following the mule track. The route briefly meets the road and follows it around a hairpin bend before resuming a more direct ascent line on a briefly surfaced track. ▸ Take the steps by a large boulder, which lead to a chapel at **Suc**. **3hr 40min**

The surrounding trees are usually laden with early season nuts, which may be found on the ground but are unlikely to be ripe.

Pass the tiny chapel and some houses to join the road. Cross the road and take the gently rising grass track in an easterly direction (do not take the concrete steps; these are Path 3). AV1 signage is visible after the track begins but is not clear from the road. This delightful track meanders along the hillside in the shade of the trees to cross a bridge over a stream. Continue along a well-engineered old road to cross the main river by an impressive stone bridge. **3hr 55min**

After crossing the bridge descend slightly to join the road, which climbs to Sassa. The route from here to Sassa and the Etoile du Berger is a steep climb, gaining approximately 500m in altitude in around 2km. You will occasionally encounter the road as the path takes a more direct line, passing through a couple of farms and hamlets en route to the Chapelle de Santa Margherita. **4hr 45min** ▸

Sadly, the chapel is locked, but its interior can be glimpsed through the windows.

The chapel at Suc

From here on the gradient eases. Traverse the hillside to pass through the next hamlet, Granges. Wooden railings support the route as you enter the open woods, now mixed with some pines, and the final fields to reach the path junction beneath the Etoile du Berger. **5hr 10min**

Take the well-made path that climbs the side of a drainage channel to reach the terrace of the **Etoile du Berger** and a warm welcome. **5hr 20min**

> **Etoile du Berger** (hotel, twin and double rooms, tel +39 340 5206774, **www.letoileduberger.it**). The lovely hotel Etoile du Berger takes its name from the local name for Venus, the first star seen in the evening sky and an indication to shepherds that it was time to make their way home, hence the shepherds' star.

STAGE 2

Sassa (Etoile du Berger) to Rifugio Coda

Start	Etoile du Berger, Sassa
Distance	7.1km
Total ascent	1050m
Total descent	250m
Grade	2/3
Time	3hr 50min
Maps	1:50,000 Instituto Geografico Centrale 9: Ivrea, Biella, Bassa Valle d'Aosta; 1:25,000 Carta dei Sentieri by L'Escursionista editore 12: Basse Valli d'Ayas e del Lys
Note	The 1:50,000 map indicates a different route that skirts along the hillside in a traversing line following the GTA (Grande Traversata delle Alpi). This is not a particularly pleasant route as the path contours along quite steep hillsides, following a well-worn groove of a path.

Today the route leaves the comforts of the Etoile du Berger 'mountain hotel' and the balmy lower Lys valley to climb into the higher mountains amid the green alpages, rocky ridges and misty mountains of the Piedmont border.

There are two routes to reach the CAI refuge: the 'Two Monts' route detailed below in Stage 2 or the shorter route via Col Portola (alternative route Stage 2A). The ridge linking Mont Roux and Mont Bechit makes for a thrilling first full mountain day and incorporates some steeper terrain (all of which is amply protected by fixed ropes, hence the designation on the maps of 'via ferrata'). Easier than Striding Edge, the 'Two Monts' route offers views and adventure that will, undoubtedly, win out on a clear day.

From the Etoile du Berger (1376m) descend to the path, following the water course below the hotel to the AV1 path from the previous day, and follow the AV1 signs to cross a bridge. Turn left and ascend to the gold mine bridge. **20min** ▸

Alternatively, follow the metalled road above the Etoile du Berger to end up at a sign and path to the interesting abandoned gold mines.

Gold has been mined in the Alps since Roman times. Although the deposits are not extensive, they

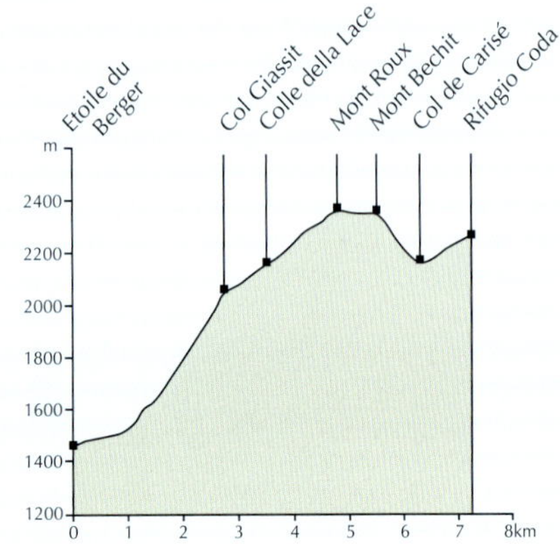
Etoile du Berger
Col Giassit
Colle della Lace
Mont Roux
Mont Bechit
Col de Carisé
Rifugio Coda
m
2400
2200
2000
1800
1600
1400
1200
0
1
2
3
4
5
6
7
8km

SR44
di-Bouroz
N
Monte Mars
2600m
Punta della Sella
2315m
0
1
km
Sassa
S
Etoile du Berger
Col Portola
F
Rifugio Coda
Col de Carisé
Mont Bechit
2320m
Mont Roux
Bec di Nona
2085m
Col Giassit
Colle della Lace
Punta Cressa
2050m

have been worth exploiting throughout history. Formed during the Alpine mountain building phase, the gold deposits are only found in the quartz veins of the host rock into which the veins were injected.

The ancient tunnels are open, so should you wish to explore the outer areas ensure a head-torch is handy. Beware – exploring anything but the first 20m or so of an old mining system can be hazardous.

From the mine, cross the wooden bridge and climb to the road. Turn right and follow the road for 75 metres to a junction. Turn right and follow the road until a sharp

The impressive footbridge to the old gold mine above Sassa

hairpin bend is reached (approximately 150 metres), where the AV1 is signed as continuing ahead. Leave the road and follow the direction of the river along a clear path. After a short distance cross a metal barrier/stile designed to deter cattle from wandering too far. Yellow arrows painted on rocks continue to clearly mark the path. As the path passes old farm buildings, it can become less obvious but always follows an uphill line. At an altitude of about 1680m a stream bed crosses the path approximately 100 metres after a stone barn. The arrows indicate continuing to the left of the stream bed (right bank in relation to the stream flow). ◂

A better route can be accessed by crossing the stream (the stream bed is usually dry in summer) and following a worn path on this side of the stream, along the line of an old wall.

Continue climbing steadily to the treeline at about 1750–1800m, where you will encounter more farm buildings. ◂ After crossing a stream, you will be able to see the cross on Col Giassit. Take the path leftwards and pass the highest farm buildings to gain the **Col Giassit** (2026m). **1hr 40min**

An overhead cable is still used for transporting items to the summer farms on the higher reaches of the mountain.

The next objective is Colle della Lace (2117m), which is visible to the left. Follow the path as it undulates along the mountainside above grazing cattle and goats from the nearby farm of Bechera before gaining the col. **2hr 10min**

A multitude of signs at the col can be somewhat confusing. None clearly indicates the AV1, although Rifugio Coda is clearly indicated with a hand-painted sign immediately left and uphill. There is also a GTA sign for Coda, Path 3; this is not a recommended route. Begin by climbing directly up the hillside as the path steepens. You will soon encounter some fixed rope to assist the nervous walker across steeper ground. The climb is quite steep for a time, and the fixed rope becomes more continuous as you reach the upper slopes of **Mont Roux** (2313m). **2hr 40min**

At no point does the route become what would normally be considered a via ferrata. The fixed rope and occasional footplates are welcome, and before long you will reach the summit where there is a visitor book in a box mounted on a pole for every intrepid walker to complete.

The descent path from Mont Bechit

Continue towards the highest point along the ridge, **Mont Bechit** (2320m). In the distance is the massive Monte Rosa chain. The path doesn't actually visit the summit of Mont Bechit. It passes across the right flank but a short detour allows the summit to be reached. **2hr 50min**

Descend from the upper slopes of Mont Bechit and follow a delightful and, in places, reasonably steep, broad ridgeline around a large cirque before arriving at **Col de Carisé** (2124m). **3hr 20min** ▸ The sign here indicates that the refuge is 25min away. Follow the path to reach **Rifugio Coda** (2252m), which is visible in the final few hundred metres. **3hr 50min**

High above the cliffs of the cirque mountain goats can sometimes be seen grazing on impossible slopes.

Rifugio Coda (CAI, sleeps 51, tel +39 015 2562405, **www.rifugiocoda.it**). This fairly small refuge, owned by CAI, is the halfway point of the Tor de Géants race. It was commissioned in 1946 and is dedicated to Delfo Coda, a partisan fighter during the Second World War who was executed by German troops in late 1944. It was conceived and designed by his father, Agostino, who was an engineer. Since the 1980s the Chiappo family have managed the hut and it retains a family atmosphere.

Mont Bechin and Mont Roux in early morning sunlight from Rifugio Coda

There are now two route options between Rifugio Coda and Gressoney-Saint-Jean since the long-awaited – and outstanding – Rifugio Barma opened in 2018. Each covers much of the same ground but both offer different challenges. Neither is easy and both involve long days, but they are a real journey through the mountains.

The optional route (stages 3A, 4A and 5A) takes in the two traditional high mountain refuges in Piedmont, Rifugio Vecchia and Rifugio Rivetti, while the main route stays in Aosta and offers more-luxurious accommodation at Rifugio Barma and La Gruba, another 'mountain hotel'.

STAGE 2A

The Col Portola Route: Sassa (Etoile du Berger) to Rifugio Coda

Start	Etoile du Berger, Sassa
Distance	4.3km
Total ascent	720m
Total descent	50m
Grade	2
Time	2hr 30min
Maps	1:50,000 Instituto Geografico Centrale 9: Ivrea, Biella, Bassa Valle d'Aosta; 1:25,000 Carta dei Sentieri by L'Escursionista editore 12: Basse Valli d'Ayas e del Lys

The Col Portola is a fine viewpoint, and this shorter alternative allows trekkers joining at Remondin to reach Rifugio Coda in a day. Another alternative is to walk from Etoile du Berger to Rifugio Barma via this short cut. Passing an unusual basin, the Plan des Sorcières (believed to be the home of a coven of witches) and traversing the mountainside to finally climb to the Col de Carisé, the route enjoys magnificent views including far-off snow-capped summits. The route is short in length but at no point is this route short of interest.

From the Etoile du Berger (1376m) join the metalled road above the hotel either by following the access track or the small path that follows the canal stream uphill. Follow the road rightwards for a short distance until you reach a well-signed path on the left next to a small building set into the steep pastures. This path is signed for Col Portola and also Rifugio Coda. There are also small, square red and white signs for the 5 Cols race (Trail 5 Colli) pointing along the same path.

Climb steadily on a rightward rising traverse through pastures and a few isolated farm buildings and cross an access track twice. The path becomes a little more

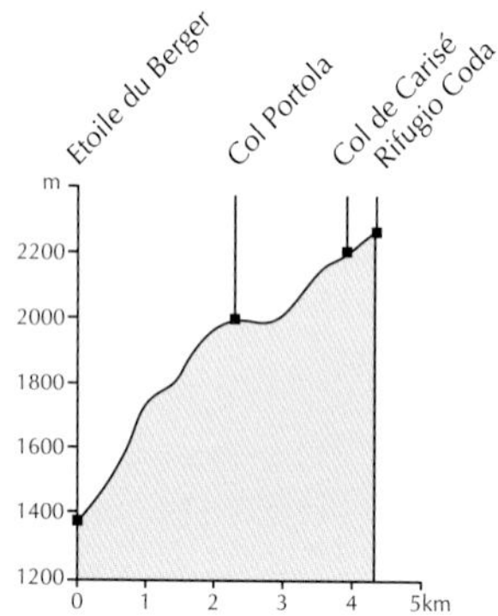

indistinct as rocks form the path near some buildings at La Goumba (1660m). Cross another access track twice in quick succession to continue climbing. (The path cuts the hairpin corner that the track takes). The next rising traverse is about 250 metres long and ends at an important but indistinct junction at a point where the vehicle track ends. **1hr 10min**

The path to Plan des Sorcières/Col Portola/Rifugio Coda takes a directly uphill route here. Care needs to be taken at this point, as you could easily end up following another path that contours around the hillside. Some arrowed waymarking indicates this path, but there is no marking for the Trail 5 Colli route.

There is less tree cover now and height is quickly gained as the route continues towards some well-maintained buildings. At these buildings trend rightwards and you will reach the plateau of Plan des Sorcières. **1hr 25min**

On the left you will see a large rock with ancient **carvings** that are reputed to represent Pleiades, a star cluster that is clearly visible with the naked eye; the stars are also referred to as the Seven Sisters, which may well be the origin of the legends that witches once inhabited the remote plateau. Other rocks on the plateau also have cupola engravings and further support the belief that ancient rites were practised here.

Continue following the path to reach **Col Portola** (1966m). **1hr 30min** An impressive view opens out in front. The refuge is visible on the skyline and Monte Mars rises impressively behind it.

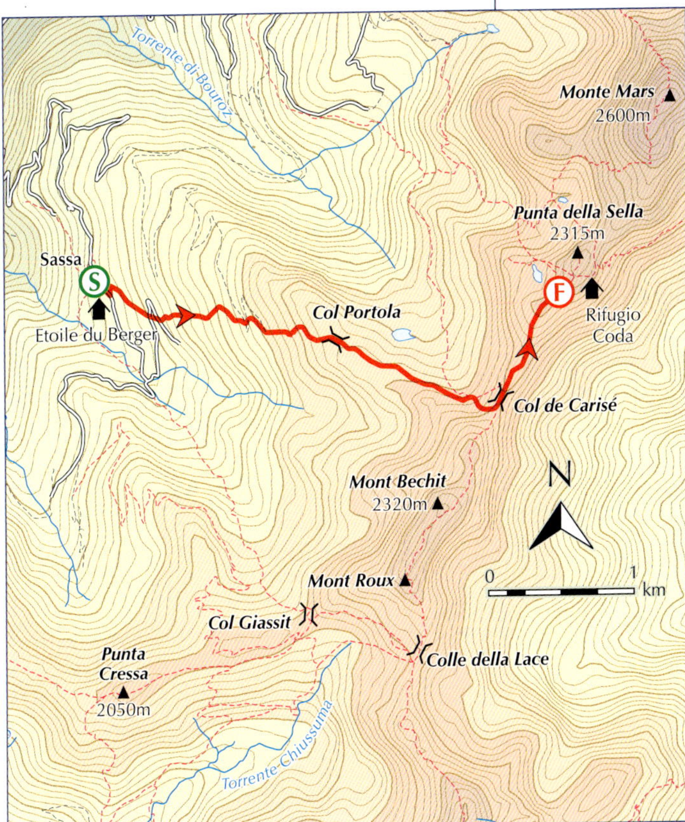

The Col Portola (1966m) with Monte Mars ahead

The warm, protected slopes just beyond the col are a perfect spot for early-ripening **mirtillo nero** (*myrtille* in France; bleaberry or whortleberry in the UK), a commonly found wild blueberry and a welcome snack! Mirtillo have traditionally been used to aid poor night vision, treat circulation problems, diarrhoea, angina and strokes. An infusion of the berries was also used to treat sore throats and mouth ulcers.

Descend a short distance before following an undulating path that rises towards the **Col de Carisé** (2124m). **2hr**

Upon reaching the col turn left and follow the path to Rifugio Coda (2252m). **2hr 30min**

Rifugio Coda (CAI, sleeps 51, tel +39 015 2562405, **www.rifugiocoda.it**).

STAGE 3

Rifugio Coda to Rifugio Barma

Start	Rifugio Coda
Distance	8.1km
Total ascent	530m
Total descent	700m
Grade	2
Time	4hr 30min
Maps	1:50,000 Instituto Geografico Centrale 9: Ivrea, Biella, Bassa Valle d'Aosta; 1:25,000 Carta dei Sentieri by L'Escursionista editore 12: Basse Valli d'Ayas e del Lys

The itinerary for Stage 3 makes for a relatively short day that traverses some wild and remote-feeling upper valleys and cirques. The mountains in the distance, principally Monte Rosa, provide a brilliant white backdrop, and high mountain chalets provide equally picturesque foreground detail for photographs today. A final climb through the Mont Mars Nature Reserve brings you to the new and well-equipped Rifugio Barma with its wide observation windows overlooking the lake. Stages 3A–5A follow th original route of the AV1 to Gressony-Saint-Jean.

From Rifugio Coda descend briefly before traversing around the hillside to an unnamed col at 2234m. Follow the path as it drops steeply and passes a number of small lakes among the rocks of the Goudin basin. Continue descending (steeply to begin with) to reach the high summer pasture and farm buildings of **Serrafredda** (1841m). **1hr 30min** ▸ Follow the AV1-marked path in a northerly direction. The path is indistinct in places but upright stones have arrows painted on them.

Clear views of Monte Rosa are the reward for an early start.

Upon reaching **Gouillas** (where a Black Madonna can be found in a small shrine in the wall of the building) take the dirt road towards the farm at Leretta. **2hr**

The high alpage of Serrafredda

Black Madonnas can be found across Europe. It is unclear as to their origin, but, according to folklore, a black statue of Mary was discovered in Jerusalem 1600 years ago and was believed to have been carved by St Luke. It was taken to Oropa (over the

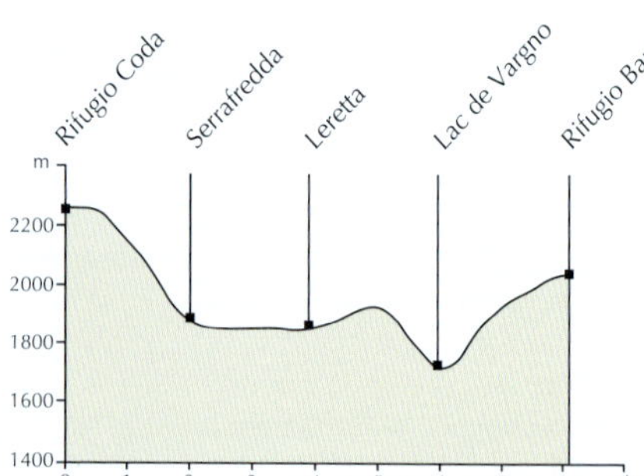

main ridge line near Biella, Piedmont) and placed in small rock alcove. A church and, later, a basilica were built. The religious complex at Oropa is still a popular venue for pilgrims.

At **Leretta**, just before the bend in the dirt road, take the small path up the hillside to the right. ▸ Climb through the thinning forest to a height of approximately 1900m before levelling out. After about 500 metres

This path junction is easy to miss as the track encourages a quickening of pace and the 1:50,000 map indicates that it follows the vehicle track.

descend to join another vehicle track. Follow this track for only about 200 metres where it becomes a footpath by a small pond. From here the path descends to **Lac de Vargno** (1664m). Follow the path and after passing some abandoned high chalets enter the forest to arrive at the dam wall. **3hr 10min**

Cross close to the dam on a good path and climb the path on the other side to join a vehicle track up to a disused building, which appears to have been part of the water management system.

Rifugio Barma is signed as being 1hr 20min away along Path 2. Climb through the old farm buildings on an exceptionally well-made path. You will reach the highest buildings along a newly built dirt road that is not shown on current maps. Continue climbing the hillside at a pleasantly gentle angle on the well-engineered path. After passing the boundary of the Mont Mars Nature Reserve, you will arrive at Lè Lounc (1942m). **4hr**

Beware that Path 2B takes a lower line while the path to the refuge continues on an upwards course. Aim for the level ground to the left of the large rock bastion above; a familiar AV1 triangular marker is a reassuring sight. At a path junction at the top of the rise there is presently no signage for the refuge but follow the signs for Path 2 and Colle della Barma and the refuge comes into view almost immediately.

The large refuge is clearly visible. Follow the path to the left of the small lake to arrive at **Rifugio Barma** (2060m). **4hr 30min** An old and privately owned building to the right of the lakes could be mistaken for the refuge.

Rifugio Barma (independent, sleeps 54, tel +39 331 1087009, rifugiobarma@gmail.com **www.rifugiobarma.it**). Being a very recently built refuge, family-run Rifugio Barma has hot and limitless showers, small dormitories and excellent food. It even accepts credit cards and has Wi-Fi.

A *barma* (French: *balme*) is a natural shelter under or behind a large rock or boulder.

STAGE 4

Rifugio Barma to Niel (La Gruba)

Start	Rifugio Barma
Distance	13.7km
Total ascent	900m
Total descent	1400m
Grade	2
Time	7hr 10min
Maps	1:50,000 Instituto Geografico Centrale 9: Ivrea, Biella, Bassa Valle d'Aosta; 1:25,000 Carta dei Sentieri by L'Escursionista editore 12: Basse Valli d'Ayas e del Lys
Note	An additional hour or so walk downhill from Niel will take you into the Lys Valley should you prefer a short expedition or if an escape route is needed.

You will cross two high passes today and visit a third as you follow the ridge. These ascents, coupled with small lakes and a mountain plateau sprinkled with tiny ponds and rare Alpine plants, make today a long day filled with a host of diverting encounters. An early start is advised if for no other reason than to ensure the delights of La Gruba are enjoyed to the full. The hamlet of Niel is worthy of an exploratory wander too.

The first major objective is Colle Marmontana (2348m). From the refuge take yesterday's path as it retraces its steps to the signpost at the small col above the rock bastion. The Colle Marmontana is marked as 1hr 35min away. Follow the path across reasonably rough ground and descend to the new dirt track, clearly visible below. The AV1 makes its own way across the hillside while the recently built dirt track takes a gentler line to reach the alpage of Marmontana (2136m). **1hr** There is little advantage in taking the direct line other than for purists. A herd of cows and their cowherd made as good a time along

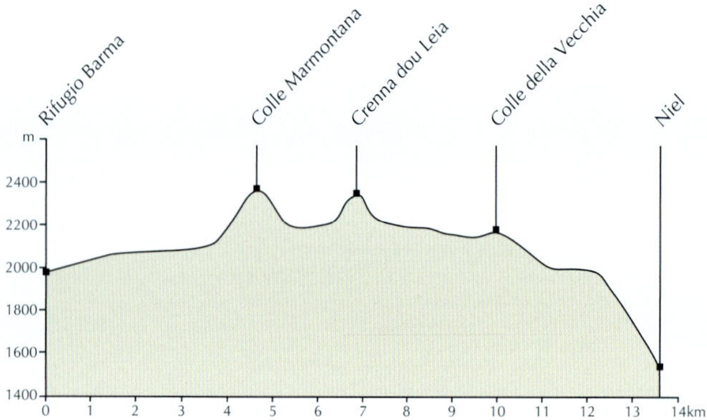

this track as the author did following the official line of the AV1.

At the alpage a path junction with Path 1B indicates the direction of Colle Marmontana (uphill above the farm buildings). Climb steadily to reach the **Colle Marmontana** (2348m). **1hr 35min** The col is surprisingly rocky and probably a good place to take a break and enjoy the view as well as identify the next sections of the stage. Kiersee, a very Germanic-sounding lake, is the next objective and care is needed for the descent as the route twists and turns down a rocky bowl. Once you reach the crystal-clear lake, cross the dam by a small bridge. ◂ Signs indicating Colle della Vecchia as being 2hr away are probably optimistic.

A minute spent here may well reveal a surprising number of brown trout in the stream.

Keep to the old wall on the left, follow it to the end before crossing the slight depression and keep a look out for some yellow markings, which may be difficult to see among the undergrowth in midsummer. You may be distracted by a path leading through undergrowth rightwards; this quickly peters out.

Having located the path, continue along the side of the valley; the path continues to be good throughout.

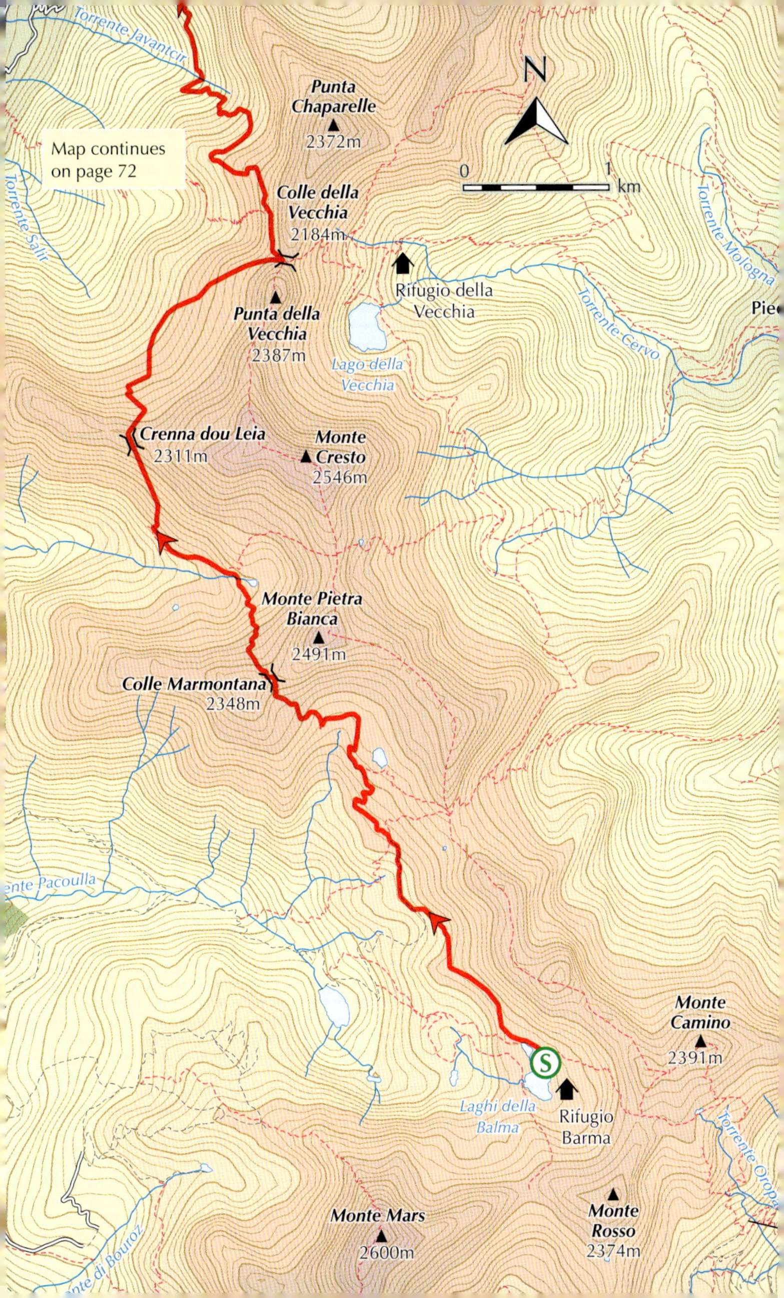

Map continues on page 72

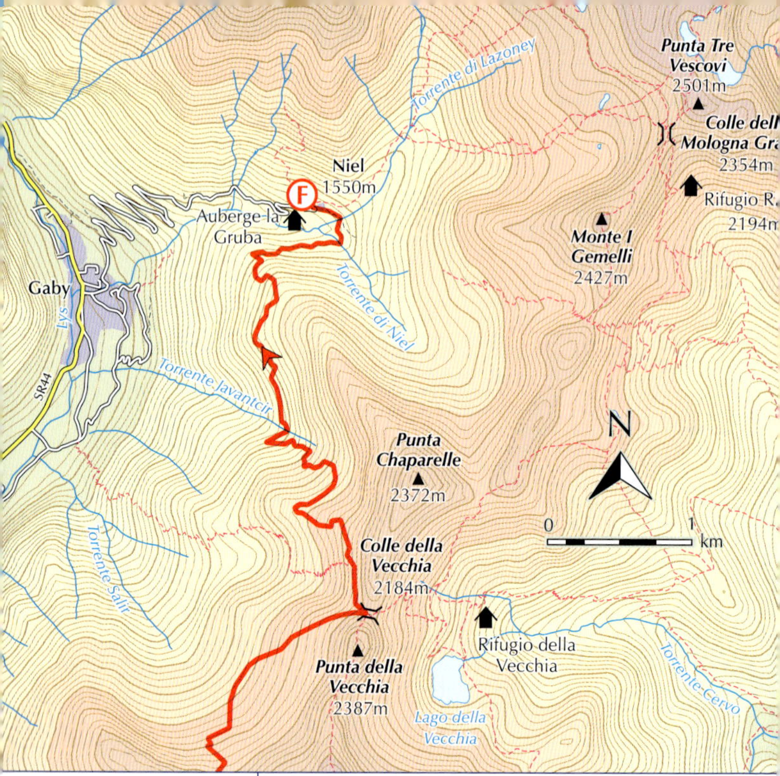

Near the Mianda chalet (little more than an old shepherd's hut) at approximately 2000m and about 20min from Kiersee, the route begins its climb to the next col. Be careful not to overshoot and miss the path as it leaves the main route, Path 3.

> As it climbs, the path edges here are smothered in **Eyebright**, a small white flower with yellow and purple markings. As the name implies, it was used to treat eye infections and other conditions.

Climb steeply, gaining a little over 300m, and in about 30min you will reach the narrow defile of **Crenna dou Leia** (2311m). **3hr 05min**

Yellow Wolf's Bane grows in the shade. It is a highly poisonous plant that can cause severe intestinal pain from even the slightest touch. Historically used to create poison arrows for wolf hunting and favoured by assassins, it is a formidable plant.

Descend steeply to reach the plateau below. The path is now predominantly on rock and gains little altitude for the next kilometre or so. ▸

This is a jumbled, rocky landscape interspersed with delightful pools alive with frogspawn and cotton grass.

Follow the path as it twists and turns endlessly on its journey to the col, which is hidden behind the rounded bulk of Punta della Vecchia, finally arriving at **Colle della Vecchia** (2184m). **4hr 35min** ▸

The estimate of 1hr 50min to Niel on the signs is an optimistic calculation.

High Alpine ponds on the plateau towards Colle della Vecchia

From the col take the obvious and well-made old mule track in a northerly direction, passing some interesting rock carvings along the way.

The two **carved female figures** greeting each other represent the two valleys joining together. In ancient times women often took on the role of mule drivers and travelled this pass to trade between the valleys.

Continue along the AV1 to join Path 8 at a path junction (1669m). **5hr 50min**

Traverse around and under the outcrop to cross the stream via a bridge and climb back up to a high point of 1750m. After passing numerous old dwellings in the forest (most of which are in a poor state of repair but allow the inquisitive traveller an opportunity to see old chalets in their unrestored state), continue descending until Niel can be glimpsed through the trees to the left.

It may be alarming to contemplate how you will cross the steep, deep valley to reach Niel, but fortunately the path contours around the hillside and crosses the stream above some cataracts on an old packhorse bridge.

Cross the packhorse bridge and follow the track into **Niel** (1550m). La Gruba is one of the first buildings on the right and is well signposted. The hotel entrance in at street level. **7hr 10min** ◂

The track becomes the 'main street', which is too narrow for any vehicles having been designed just for those travelling on foot, be it two or four.

La Gruba Hotel (private hotel, 16 beds, tel +39 340 8270110, **www.lagruba.it**). La Gruba is a delight, beautifully decorated rooms and high-quality cuisine make for a luxury getaway experience. The restaurant is popular with visitors from the valley and, with only 16 beds in total (some in shared rooms) and no other accommodation options in Niel, booking is essential.

STAGE 5

Niel (La Gruba) to Gressoney-Saint-Jean

Start	La Gruba, Niel
Distance	16.25km
Total ascent	900m
Total descent	1140m
Grade	2
Time	6hr 45min
Maps	1:50,000 Instituto Geografico Centrale 9: Ivrea, Biella, Bassa Valle d'Aosta; 1:25,000 Carta dei Sentieri by L'Escursionista editore 12: Basse Valli d'Ayas e del Lys; 1:25,000 Carta dei Sentieri by L'Escursionista editore 8: Alte Valli d'Ayas e del Lys, Monte Rosa

From lonely shepherd huts to royal mansions, this is a day of contrasts. It starts in a picturesque and remote village and finishes in an equally picturesque town, Gressoney-Saint-Jean.

The contrast between the tranquil upper valleys and the busy Lys valley will be noticeable, and the chance to restock supplies and refresh oneself will be a welcome one. You will encounter the influence of the Queen of Italy, Margherita, via the beautiful former royal residence of Castel Savoia and her love of all things mountainous. To spend the early evening in a bar in the square enjoying a well-earned drink and watching the world go by is the icing on the cake.

The AV1 (and Path 6B) is located just beyond La Gruba. Signage for Path 6B is more prevalent along this section. Take this path, a fantastic packhorse track, and follow it as it climbs out of the hamlet, quickly gaining height. ▸ After passing a few well-maintained chalets, cross a bridge **30min** and climb more steeply until you arrive at a level area, passing close to the small lake of Lac dou Grekij (2219m). **2hr**

The almost prehistoric-looking houseleek (*sempervivum*) grows in abundance along the path.

Cross a small section of Alpine wetland (the path and waymarking are less distinct for a short section but the general direction of the col is obvious). Some signs

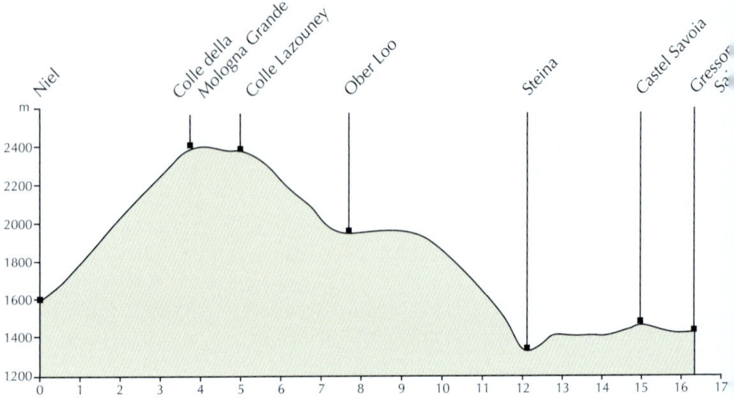

indicate that the col is 5min away, but it takes barely 2min to reach **Colle della Mologna Grande** (2354m). **2hr 10min**

Turn left and follow the signs to **Colle Lazouney** (2387m) **2hr 30min**, along a pleasant meandering path. ◂

As you reach the col, Mont Blanc is visible in the distance.

After the col the path becomes indistinct and could be difficult to follow in poor visibility. Cross a lovely, level grassy area, which has some upright waymarkers to help you keep to the path, and bear left to begin the descent of the upper Loo valley. The predominant

Departing Colle Lazouney with Mont Blanc in the background

marking is for Path 12, which takes the left-hand side of Monte Kick, a large outcrop in the centre of the valley.

Pass through **Ober Loo** (2080m) **3hr 15min** and continue down the valley. ▶ Cross the river at a bridge at Loo di Sotto (1860m) and enter the treeline on a good path. The very high iron content of the rock here is apparent in the red-brown walls at the side of the path.

Ober Loo appears to be going through redevelopment. The name hints at the origins of the language and culture that came into the valley from the Valais in Switzerland.

After you pass a crucifix, a beautiful rock table and benches, reminiscent of Aslan's Altar, offer a fantastic viewpoint into the valley below. Descend steeply from here, before crossing a bridge, and continue steadily losing height to enter the traditional Walser-style hamlet of **Steina**. **5hr 15min** ▶

An occasional bus service operates from here to Gressoney-Saint-Jean.

The **Walser** architecture and culture harks back to a bygone age. During the Middle Ages people freely travelled from the Upper Valais as the high mountain passes opened up due to glacial retreat. Glacial advances later blocked these passes once more, trapping the Valais people in these upper valleys. The large upper balconies and stilts are classic characteristics of a Walser house. The deeply darkened wood from which the chalets are built and the narrow streets are further indicators of the Walser design.

A short road section comes as something of a surprise after so many days of tranquil mountain paths, but it lasts for only a couple of hundred metres before you leave left along a track just before a road bridge. The riverside path wends its way towards Gressoney-Saint-Jean, but, as is often the case, route-finding in the lower valley is trickier than in the high mountains.

The first real sign of town life is the Weissmatten chair lift, which you will encounter on arrival at the outer limits of Gressoney-Saint-Jean; it is possible to follow the road from here into Gressoney-Saint-Jean, which will take you about 20min with pavement all the way.

The **Weissmatten chair lift** serves the Leonardo David World Championship Slalom slopes, which

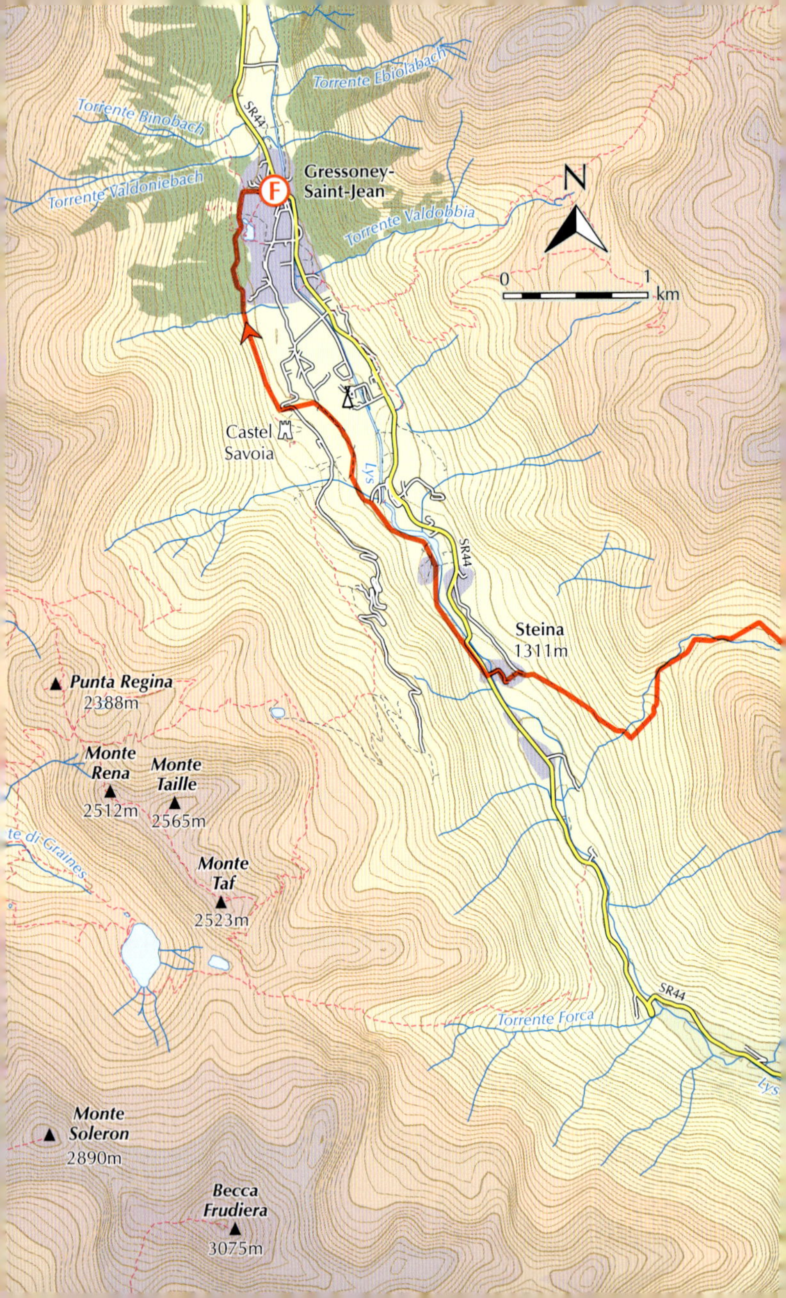

Torrente Ebiolabach
Torrente Binobach
SR44
Gressoney-Saint-Jean
F
Torrente Valdoniebach
Torrente Valdobbia
N
0
1
km
Castel Savoia
Lys
SR44
Steina
1311m
Punta Regina
2388m
Monte Rena
2512m
Monte Taille
2565m
te di Graines
Monte Taf
2523m
SR44
Torrente Forca
Lys
Monte Soleron
2890m
Becca Frudiera
3075m

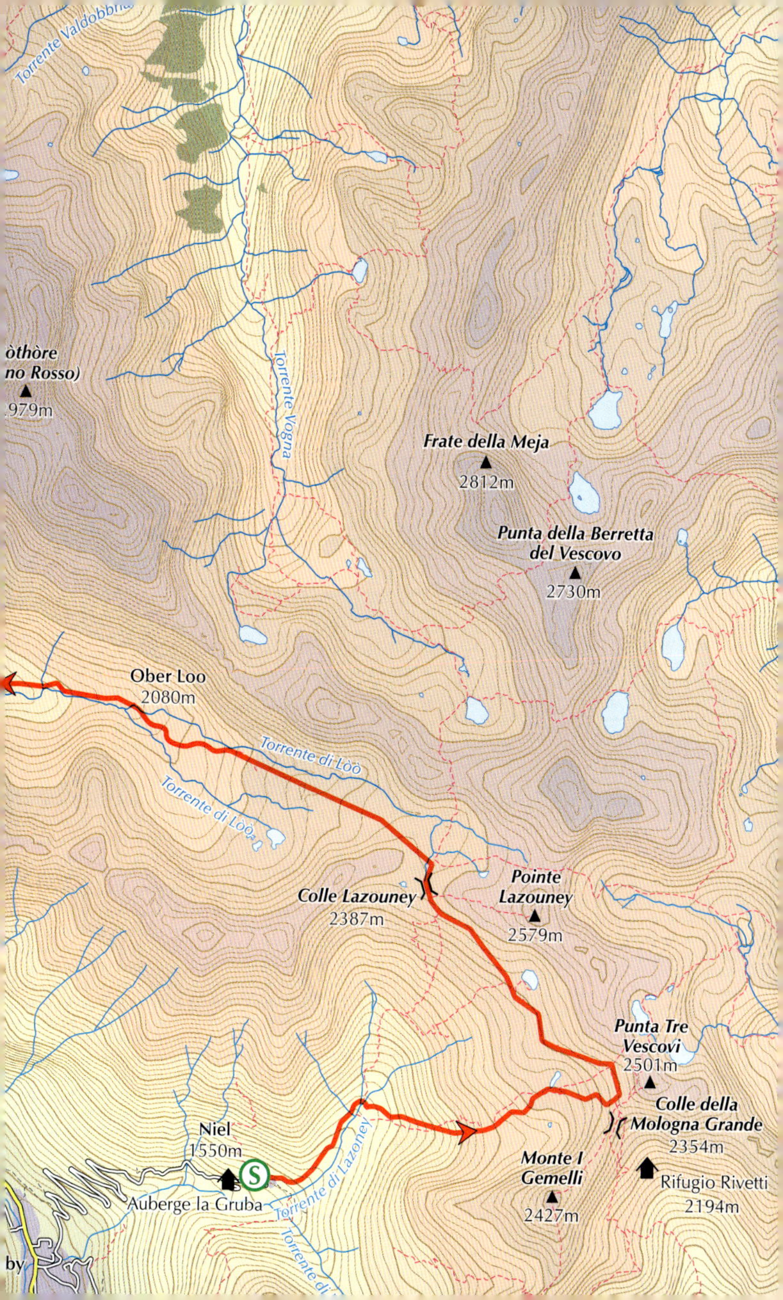

Torrente Valdobbia
òthòre
no Rosso)
979m
Torrente Vogna
Frate della Meja
2812m
Punta della Berretta del Vescovo
2730m
Ober Loo
2080m
Torrente di Lòò
Torrente di Lòò
Colle Lazouney
2387m
Pointe Lazouney
2579m
Punta Tre Vescovi
2501m
Colle della Mologna Grande
2354m
Niel
1550m
Auberge la Gruba
Torrente di Lazoney
Monte I Gemelli
2427m
Rifugio Rivetti
2194m
by

are named after a local skier destined to achieve great things but who sadly died following a racing accident in 1979 at the young age of 18.

Enter the forest about 40 metres up the ski run on the right after the first pylon of the drag lift (a waymarker is visible 20 metres into the forest). Cross a dirt road and walk beside an old wall that turns sharp left uphill. Continue to follow the wall as it turns right and joins a path that will take you uphill to join a tarmac road. The AV1 then continues on a more level route, and you will join a road for a 1min walk before an AV1 sign on a pole indicates a leftwards ascent past a 'stilt house' to come out by the entrance to **Castel Savoia**.

Castel Savoia was built in the late 1800s for Queen Margherita of Savoy, who spent her holidays in Gressoney between 1889 and 1925. Today the castle and its grounds are a popular visitor destination.

Queen Margherita had an enormous influence on the valley. She loved mountains and mountain life and changed the course of the valley's economy by making it a centre for holidays and exploration. She also became president of the Ladies' Alpine Club. Her nephew, the Duke of Abruzzi, was also an accomplished mountaineer, after whom the Abruzzi Spur on K2 is named. Her most famous namesake is probably the Margherita pizza, which reflects the Italian colours with red tomatoes, white mozzarella and green basil.

Rifugio Margherita on the summit of Punta Gnifetti is the highest in the Alps at 4556m. The queen spent a night here in 1893 to formally open the hut. It is still immensely popular today and as well as being a refuge it is also an important centre for high-altitude research.

Cross the car park to exit at the rear and follow the path uphill through trees before dropping down, crossing a small bridge and descending towards a lake, which is a

Castel Savoia, Queen Margherita's mountain hideaway

popular afternoon venue for holidaymakers in Gressoney. The path passes some stables. Take a sharp right turn and enter **Gressoney-Saint-Jean** by what feels like a backdoor route, passing a pizza restaurant (booking is advisable for an evening meal as it is a very popular place). **6hr 45min**

Gressoney-Saint-Jean has a range of essential services, including an ATM, small supermarkets and a shop that sells maps and books. The tourist information office (tel +39 0125 355185, gressoneysaintjean@turismo.vda.it), close to the large car park on the main road travelling up the valley, is a useful service for arranging accommodation, as are popular booking sites.

It is possible to continue for another half-hour up the valley on the AV1 to the two-star **Hotel Villa Tedaldi** at Tschemenoal should a night in the town not appeal.

STAGE 3A

Rifugio Coda to Rifugio della Vecchia

Start	Rifugio Coda
Distance	15.2km
Total ascent	1350m
Total descent	1730m
Grade	3 (for distance and duration)
Time	8hr 45min
Maps	1:50,000 Instituto Geografico Centrale 9: Ivrea, Biella, Bassa Valle d'Aosta; 1:25,000 Carta dei Sentieri by L'Escursionista editore 12: Basse Valli d'Ayas e del Lys

This is a long and challenging day, but high mountain lakes, rocky passes and far-reaching views mean there are plenty of distractions en route today. It is a real journey and the route crosses a number of high passes, descends to beautiful lakes and ponds, encounters farms and mountain life and includes a final rocky plateau. The ultimate destination, Rifugio della Vecchia, is a fascinating place in itself: steeped in history and legend and set in a breathtaking situation.

From the refuge descend briefly along the path before traversing around the hillside to an unnamed col at 2234m. The path drops steeply over the col. Descend and pass a number of small lakes among the rocks of the Goudin basin to reach **Serrafredda** (1841m). **1hr 30min** ◂ Follow the AV1-marked path in a northerly direction. The path is indistinct in places but upright stones have arrows painted on them.

Clear views of Monte Rosa are the reward for an early start.

Upon reaching Gouillas (there is a Black Madonna in a small shrine in the wall of the building) take the dirt road towards the farm at Leretta. **2hr**

Black Madonnas can be found across Europe. It is unclear as to their origins but, according to folklore,

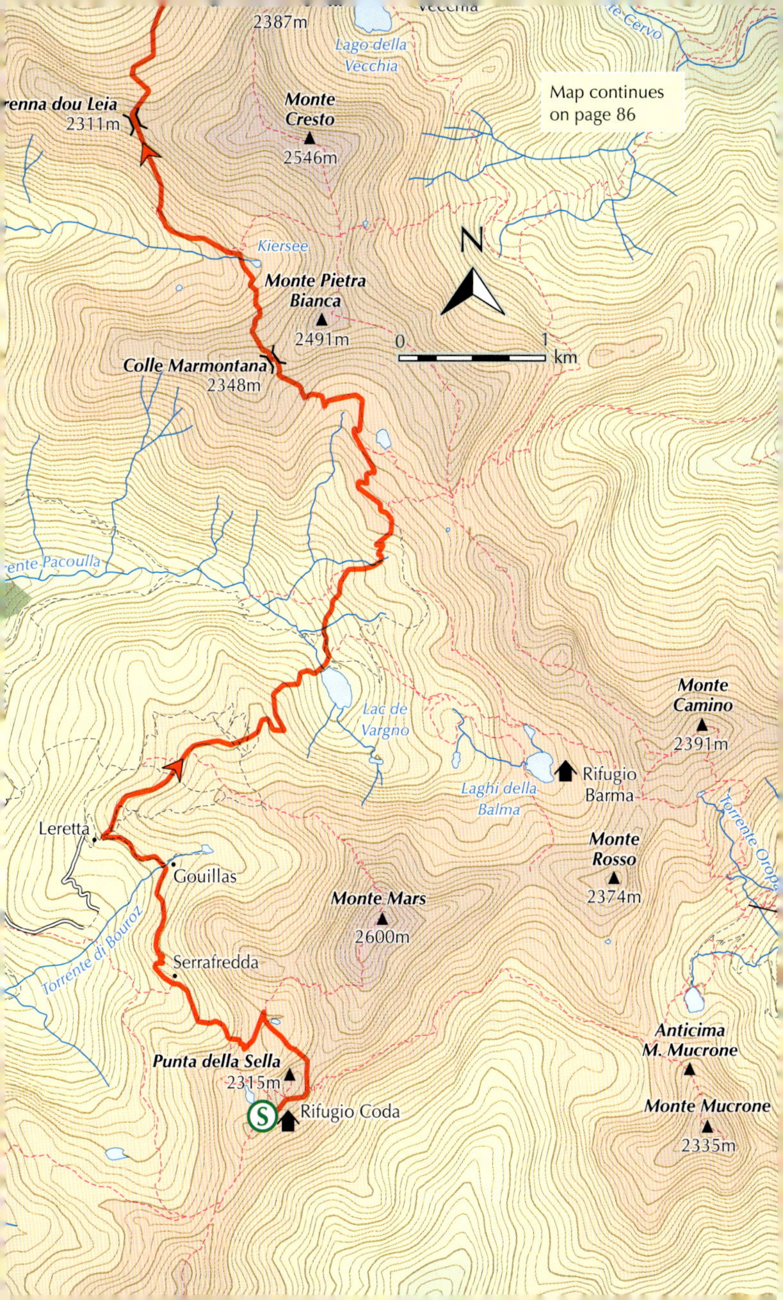
2387m
Lago della Vecchia
Map continues on page 86
renna dou Leia
2311m
Monte Cresto
2546m
Kiersee
N
Monte Pietra Bianca
2491m
0
1
km
Colle Marmontana
2348m
rente Pacoulla
Lac de Vargno
Monte Camino
2391m
Rifugio Barma
Laghi della Balma
Leretta
Gouillas
Monte Rosso
2374m
Monte Mars
2600m
Torrente di Bouroz
Serrafredda
Torrente Oropa
Anticima M. Mucrone
Punta della Sella
2315m
S
Rifugio Coda
Monte Mucrone
2335m

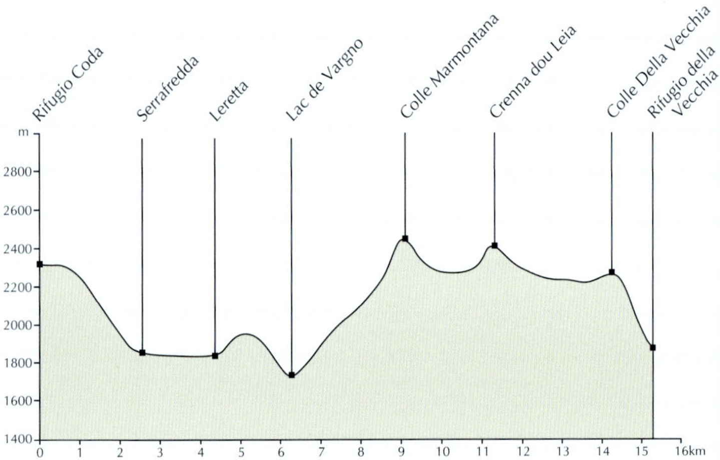

a black statue of Mary was discovered in Jerusalem 1600 years ago and was believed to have been carved by St Luke. It was taken to Oropa (over the main ridge line near Biella, Piedmont) and placed in small rock alcove. A church and, later, a basilica were built. The religious complex at Oropa is still a popular venue for pilgrims.

This path junction is easy to miss as the track encourages a quickening of pace and the 1:50,000 map indicates that it follows the vehicle track.

At **Leretta**, just before the bend in the dirt road, take the small path up the hillside to the right. ◂ Climb through the thinning forest to a height of approximately 1900m before levelling out. After about 500 metres descend to join another vehicle track. Follow this track for only about 200 metres where it becomes a footpath by a small pond. From here descend to **Lac de Vargno** (1664m) **3hr 10min** by following the path, and after passing some abandoned high chalets enter the forest to arrive at the dam wall.

Cross close to the dam on a good path and climb the path on the other side to join a vehicle track up to a disused building, which appears to have been part of the water management system.

Leretta chalet dwarfed by the mountains

There are numerous options at the path junction here. Rifugio Barma is signed as being 1hr 20min away and Rifugio Vecchia 5hr 40min away.

The next objective is Colle Marmontana (2348m). There is little reason to follow the AV1 to Rifugio Barma and on a long stage such as this time is of the essence. Walkers can use a shorter option to reach the intermediate objective of Colle Marmontana.

Path 2A begins a short distance down the track from Lago de Vargno and takes an ascending line through forest to gain a vehicle track at Grangeas (1881m); the path cuts the corners of some hairpins as it leaves the treeline. Tor des Géants signage continues to be evident. A fairly narrow path crosses a stream beneath some small cliffs and continues to climb to reach a vehicle track where you will see signage for the AV1 and Rifugio Barma. The AV1 route turns left and follows the vehicle track.

Follow the path across reasonably rough ground, taking care to watch your step, and descend to the new dirt track clearly visible below. The AV1 makes its own way across the hillside while the recently built dirt track takes a gentler line to reach the farm buildings of Marmontana (2136m). **4hr 35min**

From the alpage a path junction with Path 1B indicates the direction of Colle Marmontana (uphill above the farm buildings). Climb steadily to reach **Colle Marmontana** (2348m). **5hr 10min**

The col is surprisingly rocky and probably a good place to take a break and enjoy the view as well as identify the next sections of the stage. Kiersee, a very Germanic-sounding lake, is the next objective, and care

is needed for the descent as it twists and turns down a rocky bowl. Once you reach the crystal-clear lake, cross the dam by a small bridge. ▸ Signs indicating Colle della Vecchia as being 2hr away are probably optimistic.

A minute spent here may well reveal a surprising number of brown trout in the stream.

Keep to the old wall on the left, follow it to the end before crossing the slight depression and keep a look out for some yellow markings, which may be difficult to see among the undergrowth in midsummer. You may be distracted by a path leading through undergrowth rightwards; this quickly peters out.

Having located the path, continue along the side of the valley. At times it is hard to envisage the route but the path is present and good throughout. Near the Mianda chalet (little more than an old shepherd's hut) at approximately 2000m and about 20min from Kiersee, the route begins its climb to the next col. Be careful not to overshoot and miss the path as it leaves the main route, Path 3.

As it climbs, the path edges here are smothered in **Eyebright**, a small white flower with yellow and purple markings. As the name implies, it was used to treat eye infections and other conditions.

Climb steeply, gaining a little over 300m, and in about 30min you will reach the narrow defile of **Crenna dou Leia** (2311m). **6hr 40min**

Yellow Wolf's Bane grows in the shade. It is a highly poisonous plant that can cause severe intestinal pain from even the slightest touch. Historically used to create poison arrows for wolf hunting and favoured by assassins, it is a formidable plant.

Concentration is required now as the path descends steeply to reach the plateau below. The path is now predominantly on rock and gains little altitude for the next kilometre or so but repeatedly rises and falls in small amounts. ▸

This is a jumbled, rocky landscape interspersed with delightful pools alive with frogspawn and cotton grass.

Follow the path as it twists and turns endlessly on its journey to the col, which is hidden behind the rounded bulk of Punta della Vecchia, finally arriving at **Colle della Vecchia**. **8hr 10min** ◂

The sign indicating that the refuge is 20min away is another optimistic timing; 35min is more likely, particularly at the end of a long day.

Descend along the path losing approximately 300m. The path is marked in the more traditional Alpine red and white flashes, as the Aosta Valley, and its yellow markings, has been left behind. After passing a hermit's cave, you will arrive at the famous Lago della Vecchia (Lake of the Old Woman). Mystery and legend surround the lake (afternoon cloud will also add to the mysterious nature of the hollow).

The **legend** of the lake tells of a young local girl and a brave young soldier who fell in love and planned to marry at the lake. A nearby rock was decorated with Alpine flowers to perform the function of an altar. Wearing her best clothes, the young bride waited by the lake for a full day and night, but he didn't arrive. The following day a devastated messenger arrived stating that her betrothed had been

Carved rock depicting the legend of the lake above the refuge

killed in a hunting accident in the forests. The love of her life was buried at the bottom of the lake, and the young girl remained nearby to guard over him in the company of a bear. As she grew older and wiser, she became known as a sorceress, an expert in herbal remedies, to whom the locals would visit for help. When she died she was also buried in the lake to be with her beloved. It is believed that on a moonlit night their white ghosts can be seen flying over the lake.

The final descent takes you along a good path, past a rock carved with an image of a woman and a bear, to reach **Rifugio della Vecchia** (1872m). **8hr 45min**

Rifugio della Vecchia (private, 20 beds, tel +39 015 885 3232, valeria@rifugiolagodellavecchia.com). Vecchia is Italian for 'old woman', and the refuge owes much of its existence to women; indeed the current guardian, Valeria, has certainly added some distinctive art works to what is one of the smallest refuges in the region.

STAGE 4A

Rifugio della Vecchia to Rifugio Rivetti

Start	Rifugio della Vecchia
Distance	10.1km
Total ascent	1200m
Total descent	850m
Grade	2
Time	5hr 40min
Maps	1:50,000 Instituto Geografico Centrale 9: Ivrea, Biella, Bassa Valle d'Aosta; 1:25,000 Carta dei Sentieri by L'Escursionista editore 12: Basse Valli d'Ayas e del Lys

The first objective of the day is to climb back to the col from the day before. It's not a particularly welcome start but you are more likely to experience clear skies than the more usual afternoon mists of the previous day. It is a shorter day and the route follows some interesting old tracks for part of the way, reminding us that people have travelled these mountains for thousands of years. These paths were built, in the main, by the womenfolk of the mountains, who travelled along them to sell their wares in the Alpine foothills. The day will encompass the first of many delightful Walser hamlets, and you will climb more significant cols before reaching the beautiful little Rifugio Rivetti.

From Rifugio della Vecchia (1851m) return to the **Colle della Vecchia** (2184m). **45min** ◂ From the col the path is signed to Niel. It is an old packhorse track (originally used by women of the Lys valley to take dairy produce over to Biella as their husbands often worked away as stone masons) and is in very good condition. The estimate of 1hr 50min to reach Niel is an optimistic calculation; over 2hr is more likely.

This is often an opportunity to admire the views over the low cloud that is often present in the valleys early in the day.

Shortly before the Path 9 junction the path passes a second **carved rock**; this time two women are

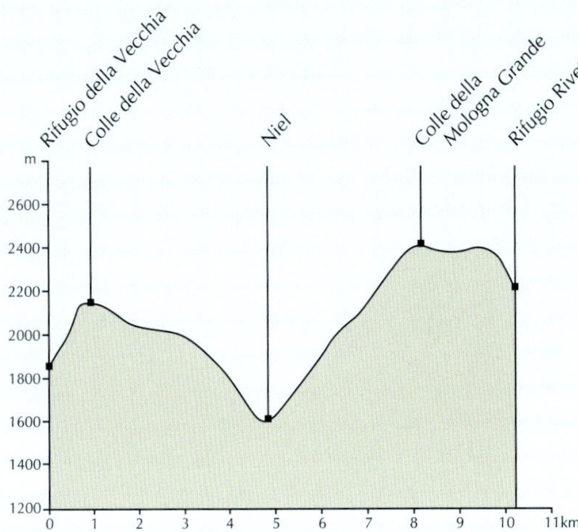

carved into the rock. They represent the two valleys that this path links at this wild and remote point.

Continue descending to reach a junction with Path 8 (1669m), close to a large rock buttress. **2hr** The path traverses under this bastion. Follow the path as it crosses a stream and climb to 1750m before descending through the forest, passing abandoned chalets en route. After approximately 50min you will be able to glimpse Niel through the trees.

It may be disconcerting to contemplate how you will cross the steep, deep valley to reach Niel, but fear not, a very handy packhorse bridge crosses the canyon saving a considerable amount of ascent.

On leaving the forest cross a picturesque packhorse bridge and enter **Niel**, 1550m. **3hr 15min**

La Gruba Dortoir and Restaurant makes for a welcome coffee stop before beginning the ascent to the Colle della Mologna Grande.

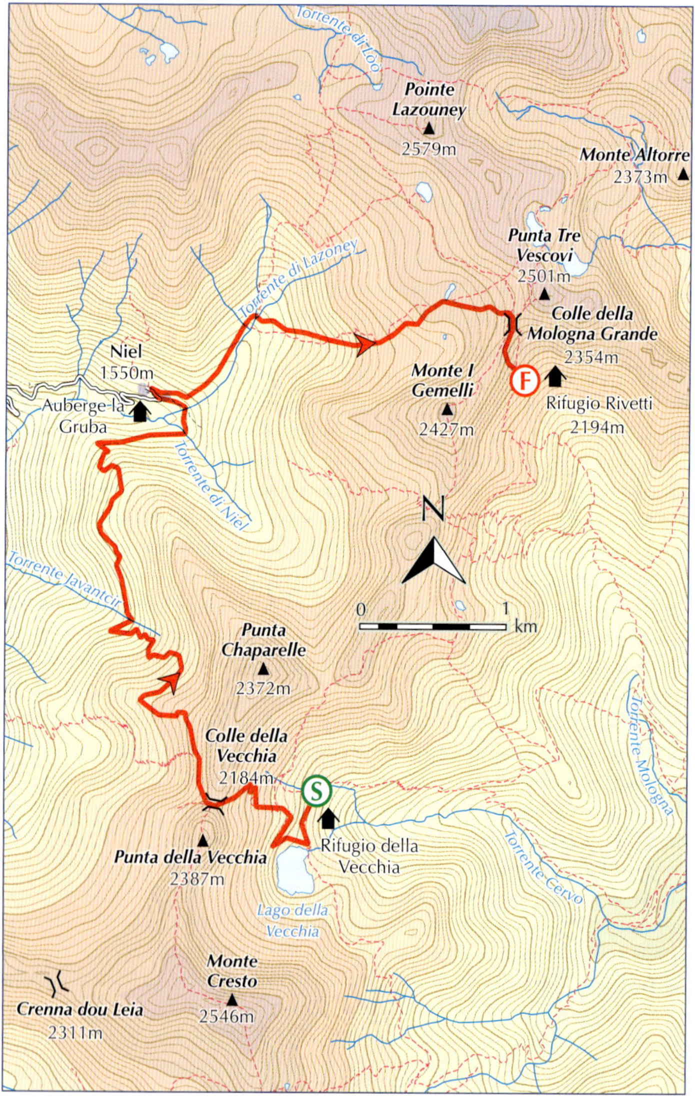
Torrente di Loo
Pointe Lazouney
2579m
Monte Altorre
2373m
Punta Tre Vescovi
2501m
Torrente di Lazoney
Colle della Mologna Grande
2354m
Niel
1550m
Monte I Gemelli
2427m
F
Rifugio Rivetti
2194m
Auberge la Gruba
Torrente di Niel
N
Torrente Javantcir
0
1
km
Punta Chaparelle
2372m
Torrente Mologna
Colle della Vecchia
2184m
S
Rifugio della Vecchia
Punta della Vecchia
2387m
Torrente Cervo
Lago della Vecchia
Monte Cresto
2546m
Crenna dou Leia
2311m

The AV1 (and Path 6B) is located just beyond La Gruba. Signage for Path 6B is more prevalent along this section. Take this path, another fantastic packhorse track, and follow it as it climbs out of the hamlet. ▸

The almost prehistoric-looking houseleek (*sempervivum*) grows in abundance along the path.

Take the AV1/6B path out of Niel, climbing past a few well-maintained chalets, and cross a bridge. The path climbs more steeply here, levelling off at around 2200m. Cross a small section of Alpine wetland (the path and waymarking are less distinct for a short section but the general direction of the col is obvious). Signs indicate that the col is 5min away; it is barely 2min! Arriving at the **Colle della Mologna Grande** (2354m) **5hr 10min**, you have little difficulty left to complete. A 30min descent to the refuge is all that remains of the day's journey. ▸ Once more the markings are red and white, and as the ground at this altitude comprises mainly rock, you need to keep an eye out for the markings.

The altitude of this col is mismarked and there is no signage for the refuge.

Follow the rocky path, keeping an eye out for the markers, and you will soon arrive at **Rifugio Rivetti** with its brightly coloured shutters. **5hr 40min**

Rifugio Rivetti's dramatic position

Rifugio Rivetti (2194m, CAI, sleeps 53, tel +39 015 247 6141, sandrozoia@libero). The refuge is well kept and, interestingly, is decorated in an unusual white and blue style inside. The central stove warms and dries out any damp kit and makes for a unique centrepiece in the cosy communal room; small *dortoirs* add to the intimate atmosphere, particularly if the afternoon mist is swirling around outside. Home-made cake and Italian coffee are a very welcome afternoon treat, adding to the sense of well-being after another day's journey.

Pack horse bridge entering Niel.

STAGE 5A

Rifugio Rivetti to Gressoney-Saint-Jean

Start	Rifugio Rivetti
Distance	13.75km
Total ascent	370m
Total descent	1100m
Grade	2
Time	5hr 05min
Maps	1:50,000 Instituto Geografico Centrale 9: Ivrea, Biella, Bassa Valle d'Aosta; 1:25,000 Carta dei Sentieri by L'Escursionista editore 12: Basse Valli d'Ayas e del Lys

Before you arrive back in the Lys valley, the delightful and gently graded Loo valley offers a peaceful opportunity to reflect on a wonderful few days in beautiful mountains. The descent from the high mountains to the valley is always a significant change: the peace of the mountains is swapped for the hustle and bustle of a busy town, the rocky path is replaced with smooth paving, the echo of the babbling brook off rocky walls changes to voices echoing around the village square. Back down in the valley you have the chance to replenish your stores and enjoy a coffee in a village square café. Italian ice cream? Another must!

The climb back to the col is familiar but the clear morning air will allow the dramatic situation of the refuge to be fully appreciated as you arrive at the **Colle della Mologna Grande** (2354m). **30min**

Follow the signs to Colle Lazouney (2387m) **50min**, which is a pleasant meandering path. ▸

As you reach the col, Mont Blanc is visible in the distance.

After the col the path becomes indistinct and could be difficult to follow in poor visibility. Cross a lovely, level grassy area, which has some upright waymarkers to aid route-finding, and bear left to begin the descent of the upper Loo valley. The predominant marking is for Path 12, which takes the left-hand side of Monte Kick, a large outcrop in the centre of the valley.

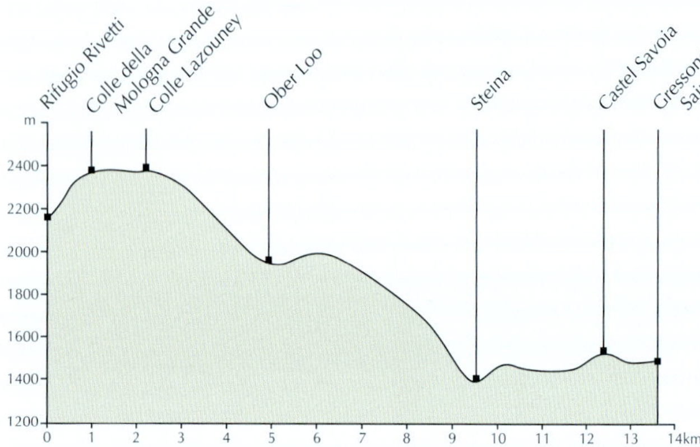

The lower Loo valley and the beginning of the forest track

Pass through **Ober Loo** (2080m) **1hr 35min** and continue down the valley. ▸ Cross the river at a bridge at Loo di Sotto (1860m) and enter the treeline on a good path. The very high iron content of the rock here is apparent in the red-brown walls at the side of the path.

Ober Loo appears to be going through redevelopment. The name hints at the origins of the language and culture that came into the valley from the Valais in Switzerland.

After you pass a crucifix, a beautiful rock table and benches, reminiscent of Aslan's Altar, offer a fantastic viewpoint into the valley below. Descend steeply from here, before crossing a bridge, and continue steadily losing height to enter the traditional Walser-style hamlet of **Steina**. **3hr 35min** ▸

There is an occasional bus service from here to Gressoney-Saint-Jean.

A short road section comes as something of a surprise after so many days of tranquil mountain paths, but it lasts for only a couple of hundred metres before you leave left along a track just before a road bridge. The riverside path wends its way towards Gressoney-Saint-Jean, but, as is often the case, route-finding in the lower valley is trickier than in the high mountains.

The first real sign of town life is the Weissmatten chair lift, which you will encounter on arrival at the outer limits of Gressoney-Saint-Jean; it is possible to follow the road from here into Gressoney-Saint-Jean, which will take you about 20min with pavement all the way.

> The **Weissmatten chair lift** serves the Leonardo David World Championship Slalom slopes, which are named after a local skier destined to achieve great things but who sadly died following a racing accident in 1979 at the young age of 18.

Enter the forest about 40 metres up the ski run on the right after the first pylon of the drag lift (a waymarker is visible 20 metres into the forest). Cross a dirt road and walk beside an old wall that turns sharp left uphill. Continue to follow the wall as it turns right and joins a path that will take you uphill to join a tarmac road. The AV1 then continues on a more level route, and you will join a road for a 1min walk before an AV1 sign on a pole indicates a leftwards ascent past a 'stilt house' to come out by the entrance to **Castel Savoia**.

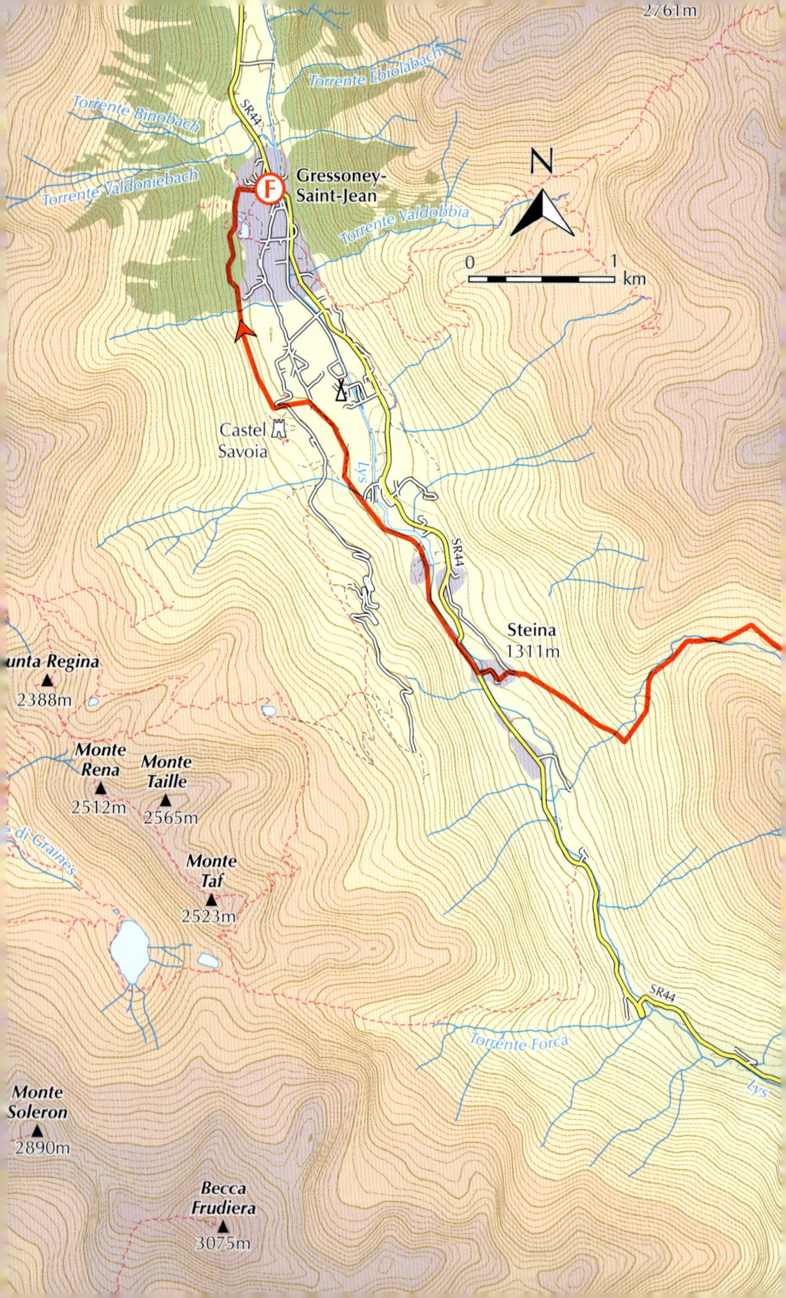

2761m
Torrente Ebiolabach
Torrente Binobach
SR44
Torrente Valdoniebach
F
Gressoney-Saint-Jean
N
Torrente Valdobbia
0
1
km
Castel Savoia
Lys
SR44
Steina
1311m
unta Regina
2388m
Monte Rena
2512m
Monte Taille
2565m
e di Graines
Monte Taf
2523m
SR44
Torrente Forca
Lys
Monte Soleron
2890m
Becca Frudiera
3075m

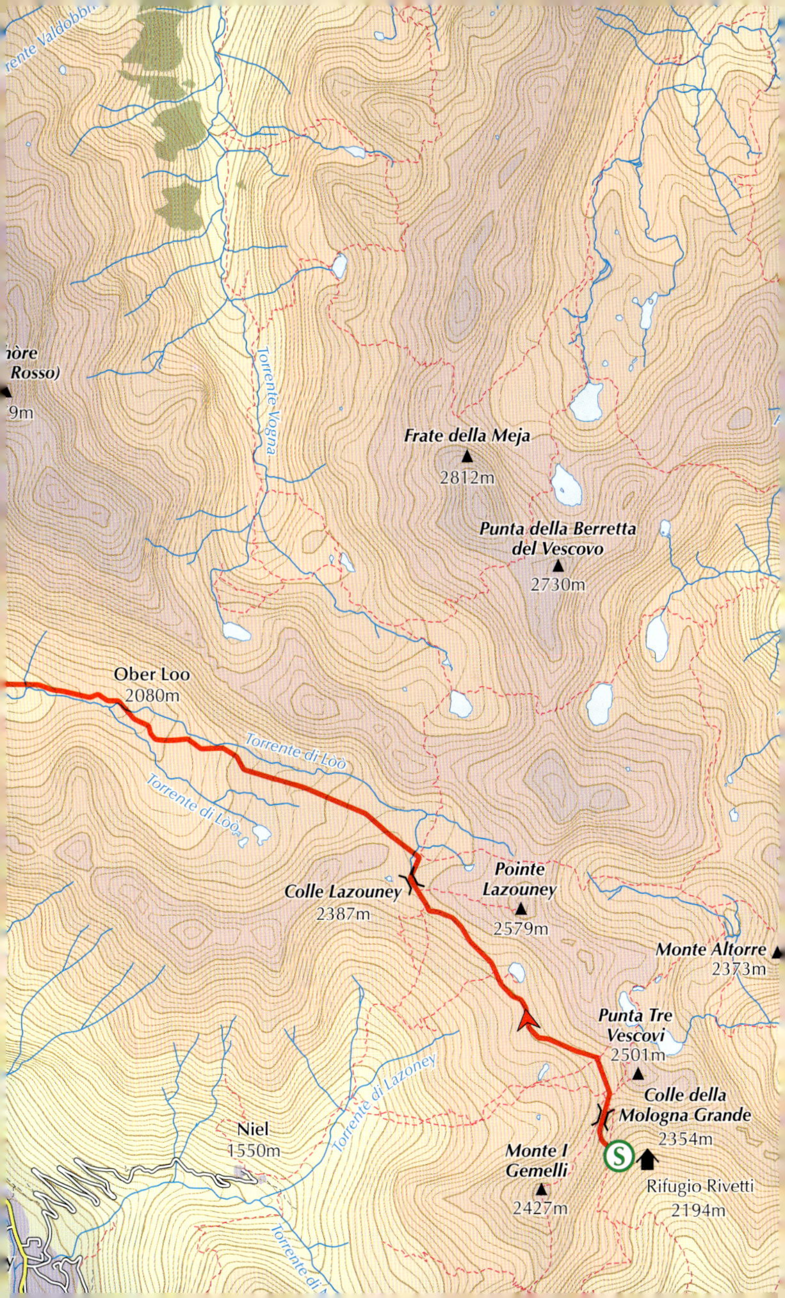

Torrente Valdobbia
Torrente Vogna
Frate della Meja
2812m
Punta della Berretta del Vescovo
2730m
Ober Loo
2080m
Torrente di Loò
Torrente di Loò
Colle Lazouney
2387m
Pointe Lazouney
2579m
Monte Altorre
2373m
Punta Tre Vescovi
2501m
Colle della Mologna Grande
2354m
S
Rifugio Rivetti
2194m
Monte I Gemelli
2427m
Torrente di Lazoney
Niel
1550m

Castel Savoia was built in the late 1800s for Queen Margherita of Savoy, who spent her holidays in Gressoney between 1889 and 1925. Today the castle and its grounds are a popular visitor destination.

Queen Margherita had an enormous influence on the valley. She loved mountains and mountain life and changed the course of the valley's economy by making it a centre for holidays and exploration. She also became president of the Ladies' Alpine Club. Her nephew, the Duke of Abruzzi, was also an accomplished mountaineer, after whom the Abruzzi Spur on K2 is named. Her most famous namesake is probably the Margherita pizza, which reflects the Italian colours with red tomatoes, white mozzarella and green basil.

Rifugio Margherita on the summit of Punta Gnifetti is the highest in the Alps at 4556m. The queen spent a night here in 1893 to formally open the hut. It is still immensely popular today and as well as being a refuge it is also an important centre for high-altitude research.

Cross the car park to exit at the rear and follow the path uphill through trees before dropping down, crossing a small bridge and descending towards a lake which is a popular afternoon venue for holidaymakers in Gressoney. The path passes some stables. Take a sharp right turn and enter **Gressoney-Saint-Jean** by what feels like a backdoor route, passing a pizza restaurant (booking is advisable for an evening meal as it is a very popular place). **5hr 05min**

Gressoney-Saint-Jean has a range of essential services, including an ATM, small supermarkets and a shop that sells maps and books. The tourist information office (tel +39 0125 355185, **gressoneysaintjean@turismo.vda.it**), close to the large car park on the main road travelling up the valley, is a useful service for arranging accommodation, as are popular booking sites.

Gressoney-Saint-Jean village square

It is possible to continue for another half-hour up the valley on the AV1 to the two-star **Hotel Villa Tedaldi** at Tschemenoal (Chemonal) should a night in the town not appeal.

STAGE 6

Gressoney-Saint-Jean to Rifugio Vieux Crest

Start	Gressoney-Saint-Jean
Distance	11.1km
Total ascent	1400m
Total descent	900m
Grade	2
Time	5hr 50min
Maps	1:50,000 Instituto Geografico Centrale 9: Ivrea, Biella, Bassa Valle d'Aosta; 1:25,000 Carta dei Sentieri by L'Escursionista editore 12: Basse Valli d'Ayas e del Lys; 1:25,000 Carta dei Sentieri by L'Escursionista editore 8: Alte Valli d'Ayas e del Lys, Monte Rosa

Today you will leave behind the Lys valley and enter the Val d'Ayas, a picturesque place with beautiful views. The route climbs to Col Pinter, one of the highest points throughout the journey at close to 2800m, while passing a number of chalets and settlements dating back to the early Middle Ages and one of the highest inhabited villages in Europe. These high mountains bring a change of vegetation and some of the less commonly seen high mountain wildflowers; mountain asters, forget-me-nots, mountain houseleeks and various gentians will brighten the hillsides as you climb the hills. Once again a number of accommodation options are available, but to pass the welcoming Rifugio Vieux Crest with its fabulous food would be a great shame.

Leaving Gressoney-Saint-Jean (1405m) means initially locating the AV1, which resumes its journey by crossing a bridge next to the car park at the upper part of town.

Cross the bridge and follow the track up the valley towards the imposing Monte Rosa chain, which dominates the head of the valley. Cross over the bridge to **Tschemenoal** (Chemonal). **30min**

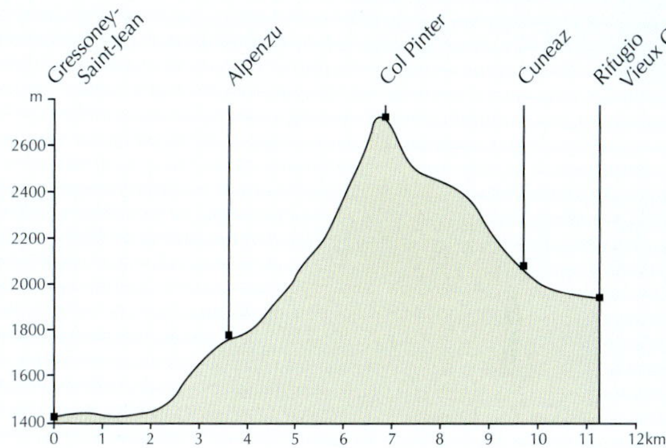

From here take the pavement for a couple of hundred metres up the valley before arriving at a sign that indicates Alpenzu is 45min away, while another states a time of 1hr 10min. The reality is probably somewhere between the two. Climb steeply through the forest and you will arrive at the hamlet of **Alpenzu** (1770m). **1hr 30min** ▸ As the path wends its way through the 13 houses that make up the hamlet (which dates back to the 1200s) the prevalent signs are for Path 6.

There are a number of signs identifying the trees along the path.

A private refuge, **Rifugio Alpenzu**, is located here (**www.rifugioalpenzu.it**).

Alpenzu was an important settlement in the Middle Ages, at a time when the German-speaking Walser people from the Swiss Valais travelled over the high mountain passes of Monte Rosa to populate these northern valleys. Some old stories claim that the snows returned to close the passes because the ancient mountain gods had been upset; however, scientists believe this to be the beginning of the Little Ice Age. Similar fables of suddenly advancing snow and ice can be found across the Alps as

explanations for the rapid glacial advance that devastated high pastures within a lifetime.

The signs for Path 6 are the most useful signs along this part of the route, although you will see an occasional AV1 triangle.

Climb diagonally up the hillside along Path 6 to pass Montil (1953m), which is little more than a few chalets. ◄ Gain the treeline and pass into the forest, continuing to climb throughout. You may be able to glimpse the objective, Col Pinter, high above at the head of the valley. You will also see some GSW (Grande Sentiero Walser) signs along this section; all the routes follow the

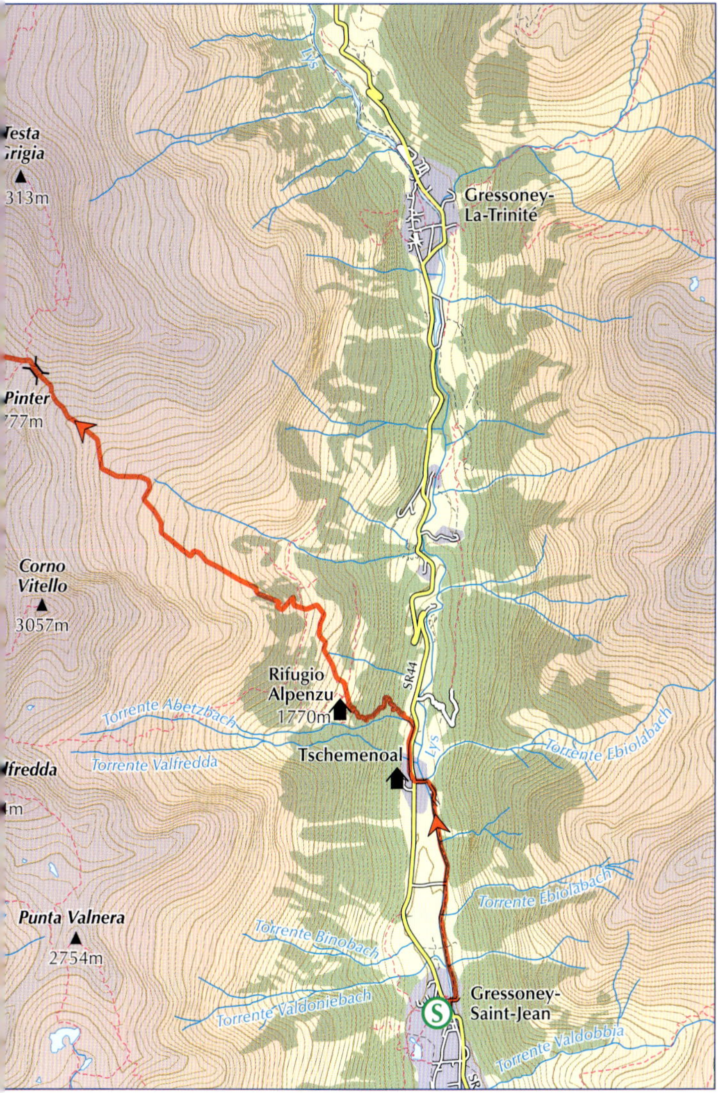
Testa
Grigia
313m
Gressoney-
La-Trinité
Lys
Pinter
777m
Corno
Vitello
3057m
SR44
Rifugio
Alpenzu
1770m
Torrente Abetzbach
Torrente Valfredda
Tschemenoal
Lys
Torrente Ebiolabach
lfredda
m
Torrente Ebiolabach
Punta Valnera
2754m
Torrente Binobach
Torrente Valdoniebach
Gressoney-
Saint-Jean
Torrente Valdobbia

The echoing cow bells can often be heard right across the valley.

same path to the col. Across the valley you will be able to spot a fascinating farmhouse tucked into the cliff, perfectly protected from winter avalanches. ◂

As you continue to climb, pass various high mountain chalets and enter the high valley. The ground steepens towards the col, which you will eventually reach – the thinner air being more apparent up here – before arriving at the summit of **Col Pinter** (2777m). **3hr 50min**

The path down from the summit is steep to begin with. Follow it carefully to a path junction where the AV1 bears left. The familiar triangular signs are present here. A narrow section has rope handrails to help walkers as it is particularly steep, although steps are present to help you descend this section. The angle of the path then starts to lessen. Continue along the path to reach **Cuneaz** (2057m). **5hr 20min** The ski station at Crest is visible in the distance.

Cuneaz is a fascinating place and one of the highest permanently inhabited villages in Europe.

◂ The route through the village is signed, although the old buildings may be enough of a distraction for you to lose track of the route. Before the restaurant take a sharp left turn and pass the Ronda building (where the village children were once taught) and the substantial (for such a small place) chapel before continuing towards Crest. The AV1 continues above the valley bottom, enjoying a fine view ahead. As you reach **Crest 5hr 50min**, a multitude of tracks can be somewhat confusing.

The Vieux Crest 'mountain hotel' is located about 50m in altitude and a couple of hundred metres distance below the ski station; there is no need to climb to the obvious buildings. When you reach a bend in the vehicle track, the best route is to turn left downhill (quite steeply) for a short distance. Opposite a small bridge on the left there is a narrow path on the right that passes a large larch tree close to a small shrine. Take this little path. It rises a little before descending to Crest. The Rifugio Vieux Crest is signed along the narrow road, about 20 metres away.

Rifugio Vieux Crest comes into view

Rifugio Vieux Crest (private, 36 beds, tel +39 0125 307983, info@refugevieuxcrest.com **www.lavarets.it/rifugio-alpino-vieux-crest**). This refuge has a very special ambience. More of a hotel than a traditional refuge, it offers small rooms (although they are likely to contain bunks and may be shared rooms), good showers, a high-quality menu and a well-stocked and varied bar.

STAGE 7

Rifugio Vieux Crest to Rifugio Grand Tournalin

Start	Rifugio Vieux Crest
Distance	9.5km
Total ascent	1020m
Total descent	450m
Grade	2
Time	4hr
Maps	1:50,000 Instituto Geografico Centrale 5: Cervino Matterhorn e Monte Rosa; 1:25,000 Carta dei Sentieri by L'Escursionista editore 8: Alte Valli d'Ayas e del Lys, Monte Rosa

This is quite a short day during which the early morning balcony path offers fabulous views of Monte Rosa and the distinctive summit of the Matterhorn. A couple of refuges are based towards the head of the valley, so it is feasible to complete part of this route in conjunction with the previous day's route, although this would be quite a long day. It is also possible to combine this stage with the following one to arrive in Valtournenche in one long day.

The Matterhorn graces the early walker with tantalising glimpses between the trees and is often clear of cloud in the morning.

You may encounter early morning milk churns sitting by the trackside awaiting collection by the ubiquitous 4x4.

From the refuge turn left along the old road that leaves the village with a short climb past a church. After about 5min join the waymarked path and then a vehicle track that offers easy walking to the hamlet of **Sousun** (1951m). **35min**

◂ At Sousun follow the track around the long curving bend to reach the hamlet and then take the track between the houses. Arrows indicate an uphill climb passing the church to the right. Follow an indistinct old track directly up the hillside for a short distance until better waymarking resumes. The newer vehicle track is easy to follow. ◂ You will reach the ski station of Champoluc shortly, where there is the option to cut a corner of the AV1 to arrive at the village of Saint-Jacques-des-Allemands by following

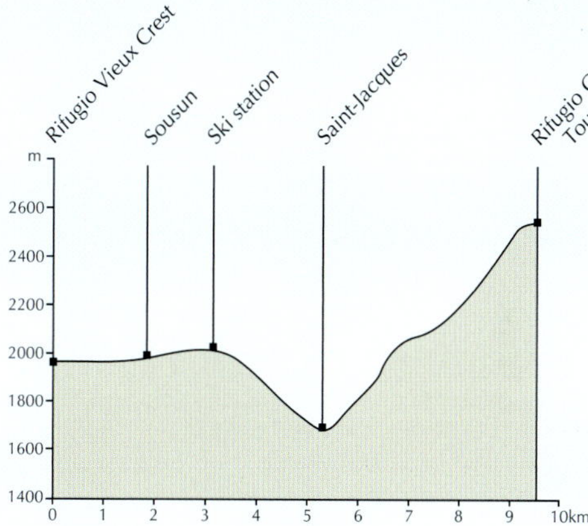

the AV1 under the funicular railway bridge to a junction with a dirt road suitable for 4x4s. Ignore signs for the refuges and follow the track downhill. This descends quite steeply along a number of switchbacks until it joins a metalled road near the valley bottom. Follow the road rightwards and downhill to join the main road and continue on this road for a couple of hundred metres into **Saint-Jacques** (1689m). **1hr 30min**

The village of **Saint-Jacques** sits at the head of a valley that was once the heart of the Germanic population that settled here from the Swiss Valais; indeed the full name for the village was once Saint-Jacques-des-Allemands, although it is now known as simply St Jacques. The valley is also known for its production of wooden clogs known as 'sabots'.

The village offers limited accommodation options, as it is an access point to the mighty 4000m mountains of the Monte Rosa chain.

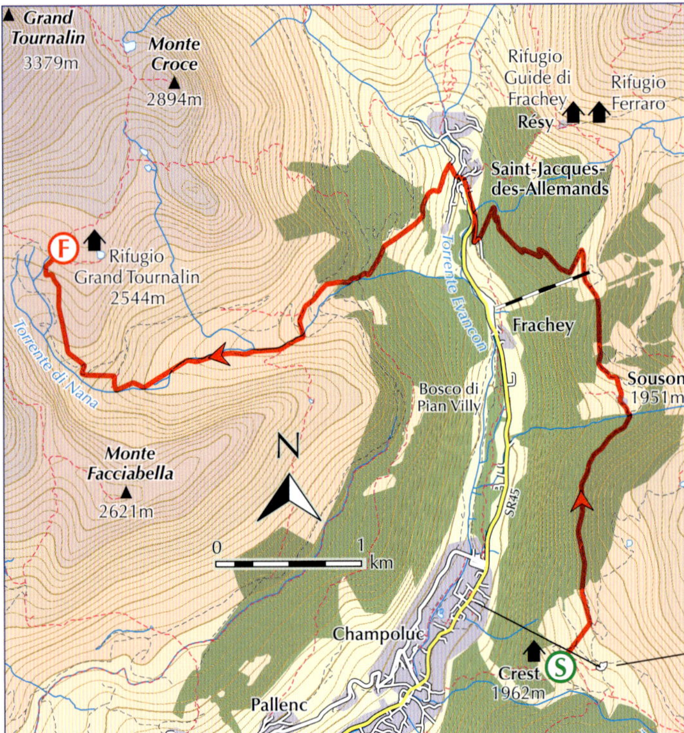

Alternative route via Rifugio Ferraro and Rifugio Guide di Frachey

Alternatively, if you choose not to follow the dirt road, the official AV1 continues to the two refuges of Rifugio Ferraro and Rifugio Guide di Frachey, which are feasible alternatives to Rifugio Vieux Crest, particularly if you spent the night before at Rifugio Alpenzu. They can be reached within an hour and a half, and from there you descend to Saint-Jacques on the AV1 path.

The AV1 is well signposted from the heart of the village and Rifugio Grand Tournalin is indicated as being

2hr 20min away. Climb out of the village passing traditional balconied Walser-style houses along the way. The path cuts the corners off the gentler vehicle access track to the high pastures, follows a stream for a while and offers increasingly impressive views of the Monte Rosa chain. As you reach the treeline (and a track to Nana, which is the name for the col, the river and a small settlement), follow the track, passing some well-appointed, recently refurbished chalets, and then continue along the bank of the Nana river/stream. ▸

It is possible to follow the vehicle track as it wends its way to the refuge, but the stream path makes for a more enjoyable route.

Cross the stream by way of a small bridge and pass the working farm of Tournalin Inferior before crossing the track on a tighter line and arriving at **Rifugio Grand Tournalin** (2544m). **4hr**

Rifugio Grand Tournalin (private, 45 beds, tel +39 0125 307003, **www.rifugiograndtournalin.com**). The refuge is hidden from sight until it is quite close by and is a welcome sight after the long uphill walk from the valley bottom. The large windows and remote nature of the refuge's position at over 2500m will be best appreciated once the day visitors have returned to the valley either on foot or, more increasingly, on electric-assisted mountain bikes.

Gaining height above Nana, with the eastern summits of the Monte Rosa chain behind

STAGE 8

Rifugio Grand Tournalin to Cretaz, Valtournenche

Start	Rifugio Grand Tournalin
Distance	7.6km
Total ascent	300m
Total descent	1300m
Grade	2
Time	3hr 30min
Maps	1:50,000 Instituto Geografico Centrale 5: Cervino Matterhorn e Monte Rosa; 1:25,000 Carta dei Sentieri by L'Escursionista editore 8: Alte Valli d'Ayas e del Lys, Monte Rosa

This short stage enjoys spectacular views from the high pass of Col des Fontaines at 2695m. In the high, rocky cols the eagle-eyed trekker may well spot ibex and chamois. You will also encounter another high mountain settlement at Cheneil, which was a base for the production of Fontina cheese. What's more, Edward Whymper stayed in the hotel in Cheneil during his observation expeditions to try to identify routes to the summit of the Matterhorn. The final descent takes you via Cretaz, once a village in its own right that, at times, seems to have been left in the 1800s, but which is now part of the larger village of Valtournenche. Communal laundry sinks and narrow lanes make the modern facilities of the upper village seem almost out of place.

Arriving in Valtournenche before lunch allows for either a restful afternoon or, should you prefer to add on the following stage, a walk of about 6hr to Rifugio Barmasse. A bus service to the main Aosta Valley operates, allowing this to be the end point for those planning to break the AV1 into two stages. This is also the final valley in which Trek-Bus operates.

From the refuge drop down onto the vehicle track and begin the ascent towards the Col de Nana.

▸ Leave the track opposite the kennels (there is also a signpost identifying the path to Col de Nana) and begin to climb before traversing the hillside towards a seemingly impossible rock barrier. Some well-built stone steps, exposed at times, wend their way through the barrier without difficulty and continue to Col de Nana (2775m). **40min** ▸

The farm dogs may well be heard barking from their kennels built into the large boulder on the left.

This high mountain col offers opportunities to spot the elusive ibex and chamois that live on these slopes in the summer.

Cloud permitting, there are also fabulous views across the Aosta Valley towards Gran Paradiso and, in the far distance, the Vanoise National Park in France. The two **national parks** of Gran Paradiso and Vanoise twinned in 1972 and worked together to reintroduce ibex (*bouquetin* in French) to the Vanoise. Together they form one of the largest protected environments in Europe and the largest in the Western Alps.

The route continues over the col. Pass a tranquil lake, perfect for wild camping as it is over the 2500m contour and therefore permitted, before reaching the stupendous

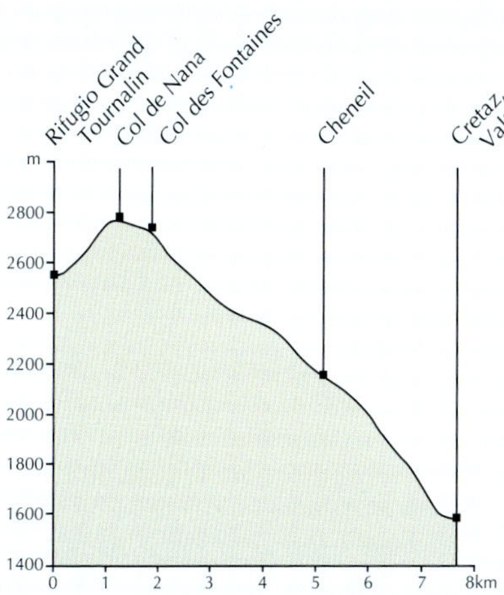

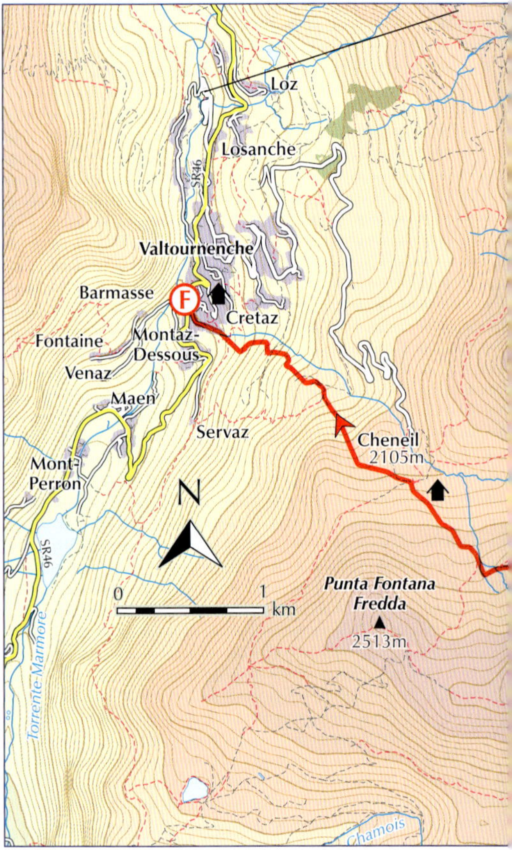

views offered at **Col des Fontaines** (2695m). **1hr 15min** It is also possible to identify parts of the upcoming days' routes from here. The descent from here is a long one, losing approximately 1200m in altitude on the way to Cretaz and Valtournenche via Cheneil. The plain of Champ-Sec provides a short respite for aching knees brought on by the descent. Continue descending and enter the forest, which is predominantly larch. ◀ After

Along the path you will spot Alpenrose, a species of rhododendron commonly found in the Alps.

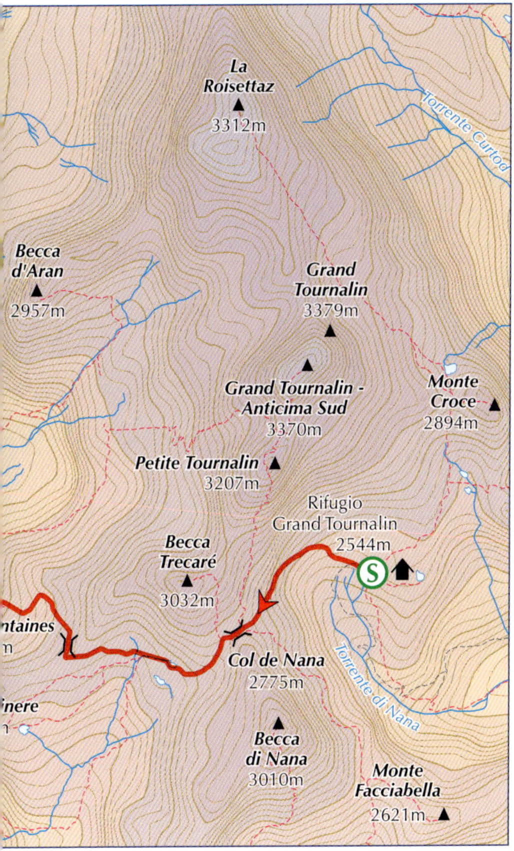

completing a final steeper section you will enter **Cheneil** (2105m). **2hr 25min** ▸

Refreshments are available from the hotel.

Leave the village on a steep path to the west, which is clearly signed from the information board. Continue through the trees to pass through Promindoz, a collection of a few houses that gets its name from words from the local patois that mean forest clearing (*pro* – lawn, *mindo* – clean), which took place in medieval times to create new

The view from Col des Fontaines; Rifugio Barmasse is to the left of the dam wall

farmland. The path becomes a mule track and continues towards Cretaz, part of the village of Valtournenche; the forest gradually changes to hardwoods as you get closer to the valley bottom. Enter **Cretaz**. **3hr 30min**

> The village square in **Cretaz** still has communal laundry sinks in a small public square. On a wall, there is a plaque commemorating the village's most famous son, Luigi Carrel, a mountain guide (not to be confused with Jean-Antoine Carrel, the second person to climb the Matterhorn and a contemporary of Whimper). The Carrel name has been associated with mountain guides in Valtournenche from the earliest days of guided exploration to today.

The Alta Via is going through some rerouting at the time of writing, and the newer signage seems to be drawing trekkers into the heart of the village of Valtournenche rather than passing by its lower side as indicated on most maps. However you reach the main road, the main village amenities lie towards the upper part, to the right.

Ancient chalets in Cretaz; communal laundry facilities

A couple of small supermarkets, the tourist information office (**www.cervinia.it/en/inverno/home-valtournenche**), a bank and an ATM will all be welcome to trekkers; a range of cafés, restaurants and accommodation options are also welcome. A pharmacy (towards the lower, Cretaz, part of the village) may also be of use.

At the point where the minor road from Cretaz joins the main road, the AV1 is located a few tens of metres downhill, opposite the pharmacy; it then descends further to cross the river before beginning to climb up to Rifugio Barmasse. More recently, the AV1 has been re-signed to exit via a bridge over the river higher in the village. Both options will ultimately lead to the same track to Rifugio Barmasse, but a few minutes spent exploring the exit route in the afternoon/early evening will pay dividends the following morning.

WESTERN SECTION

STAGE 9

Cretaz, Valtournenche to Rifugio Barmasse

Start	Cretaz, Valtournenche
Distance	4.2km
Total ascent	700m
Total descent	0m
Grade	2
Time	2hr 10min
Maps	1:50,000 Instituto Geografico Centrale 5: Cervino Matterhorn e Monte Rosa; 1:25,000 Carta dei Sentieri by L'Escursionista editore 8: Alte Valli d'Ayas e del Lys Monte Rosa; 1:25,000 Carta dei Sentieri by L'Escursionista editore 6: Valpelline St Barthélemy; 1:25,000 Carta dei Sentieri by L'Escursionista editore 7: Valtournenche, Monte Cervino, Val d'Ayas ovest

Although this is a short stage it passes through some interesting places en route to a lovely refuge situated close to the reservoir at Barmasse. Recent footpath signage changes can be slightly confusing in Valtournenche but, ultimately, the route involves crossing the river before beginning the ascent to the refuge.

Take the 'old AV1', opposite the pharmacy, which initially follows a small road for about 20 metres before continuing along another small path that drops to the left and joins a road. This road crosses the bridge and a pretty waterfall before climbing past the tiny Chapelle Madonna di Lourdes tucked under an enormous rock. Continue to a small car park that serves the local residents of Fontanaz. **25min**

Signage for the AV1 is sparse here but a well-made pavement and flight of steps to the right of some water troughs indicate Path 6. Take this as it ascends through the village (a waymark is particularly apparent on a metal pole at the top of the steps). ▶ After turning right at the top of the steps, continue for about 20–30 metres before turning sharp left and climbing straight up the hillside in dappled shade to a junction with Path 6. **50min**

It feels as if the path is passing through private grounds as it wends its way out of the hamlet.

Continue climbing up the hillside until you reach the fascinating remains of a supply rail track used for the construction of the dam built to create the reservoir of Lago di Cignana. Pass this to follow a well-engineered path, which climbs rightwards. After passing a cross, you will reach the higher valley and the deserted hamlet of

Above Falegnon on the well-used path to the refuge

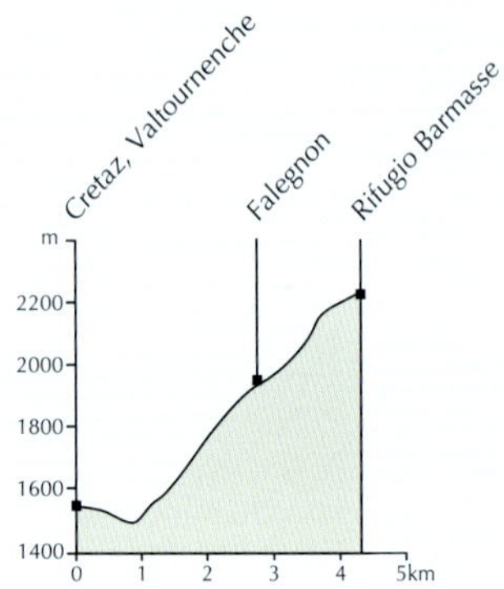
Cretaz, Valtournenche
Falegnon
Rifugio Barmasse
m
2200
2000
1800
1600
1400
0
1
2
3
4
5km

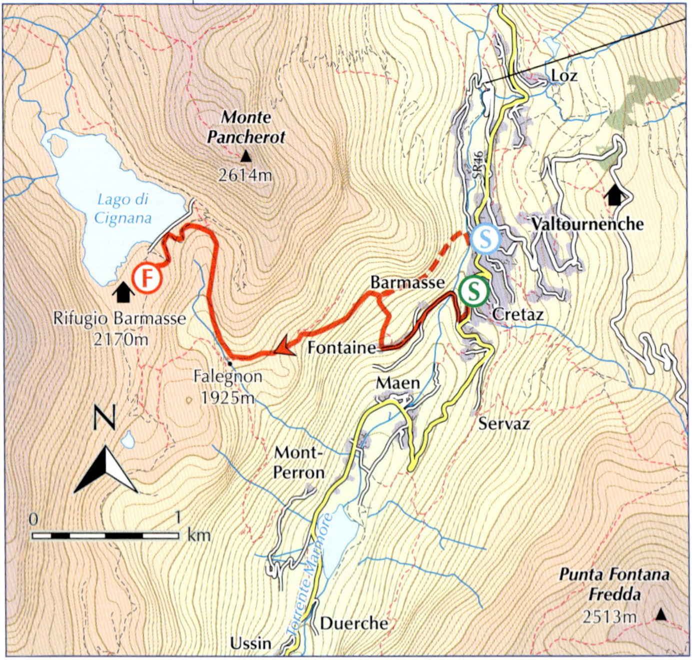
Monte Pancherot
2614m
Lago di Cignana
Rifugio Barmasse
2170m
Falegnon
1925m
Barmasse
Fontaine
Loz
SR46
Valtournenche
Cretaz
Maen
Servaz
Mont-Perron
Torrente Marmore
Duerche
Ussin
Punta Fontana Fredda
2513m
N
0
1
km

Falegnon (1925m). **1hr 30min** Continue along the well-used path towards the enormous dam wall, which only comes into sight relatively late in the trek. Traverse leftwards beneath the overshadowing structure to join a vehicle track and a welcome level section that will take you to the dam wall. **2hr**

Cross the small bridges near the chalet-styled water administration building and follow the access track for a short distance before cutting a straighter line up the hillside on a small path to reach **Rifugio Barmasse** (2170m). **2hr 10min**

The refuge works in partnership with Rifugio Cunéy (the following night's refuge), and bookings can be made for both refuges via the same website.

Rifugio Barmasse (private, sleeps 25, tel +39 345 1081551, **www.rifugiocuney.it/it/il-rifugio-barmasse**). With vehicle access and some electrical connectivity, the refuge is quite well resourced. Some shower facilities are available as well as good food and one of the best Italian hut breakfasts you will encounter. The refuge is a popular day-walk destination and also a possible staging post for the TDC (Tour des Combins), which means it is quite busy but fortunately most of the trade is just passing custom, and things quieten down in the late afternoon. Early booking is recommended, though.

STAGE 10

Rifugio Barmasse to Rifugio Cunéy

Start	Rifugio Barmasse
Distance	14.2km
Total ascent	1200m
Total descent	650m
Grade	2/3 (old, hard snow may be present)
Time	7hr 05min
Maps	1:50,000 Instituto Geografico Centrale 5: Cervino Matterhorn e Monte Rosa; 1:25,000 Carta dei Sentieri by L'Escursionista editore 6: Valpelline St Barthélemy

This is a long stage that takes you over some of the highest passes on the AV1 before finishing at Rifugio Cunéy, a basic refuge in a remote valley that is also home to the impressive Santuario di Cunéy. The 'official' time for this route is 6hr 15min but this seems a little quick. You will likely have to cross a couple of semi-permanent snow patches in the final approach to the refuge.

From the refuge follow the vehicle track for about 500 metres before taking the path to left, away from the inviting track. ◂ The path and track meet again at the summer chalets of **Cortina**. **20min** The AV1 leaves the track shortly after the chalets, but it is preferable to continue following the track. While the path takes a more direct line down the hill again, here it is indistinct and saves little time. The map shows that the AV1 takes a reasonably big diversion below the track and then climbs back to the track a short while later. It appears the diversion was made to avoid possible rockfall in the basin, but signs now indicate that walkers should continue along the track. On entering the forest keep an eye out for the signpost for the first significant col of the day, Finestra d'Ersa. **1hr 05min**

It is possible to continue along the track, but it meanders somewhat compared to the more direct footpath.

Take this path to the right to pass through the old buildings of **Fornace** (also referred to as Ersa Dessus).

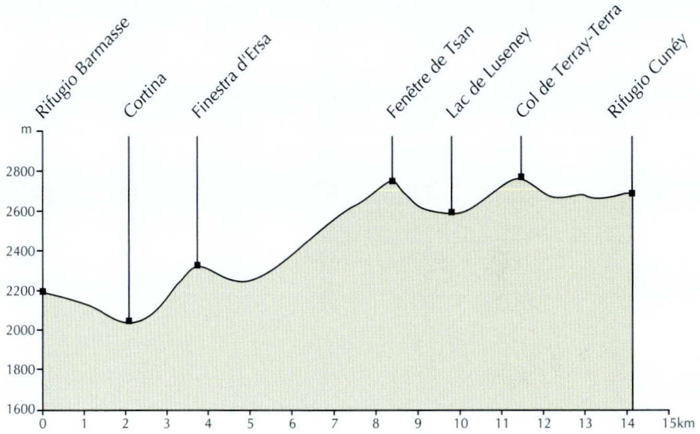

From here some of the last real views of the Matterhorn will be had before you reach the col of **Finestra d'Ersa** (2290m). **2hr**

Unusually, the path continues to ascend from the col, bearing rightwards for a short time before descending to a vehicle track. Follow the path as it climbs briefly and then descends to join the track below. Continue along the track for a couple of hundred metres before breaking off to the left and climbing along an indistinct path (although it does have painted signs on prominent rocks along the way).

It appears that the Tor des Géants keeps on the vehicle track along this section to then rejoin the path.

▸ Keep climbing along the path, passing a couple of reasonably exposed stream crossings, to eventually reach Grand Dreyere cow sheds (The sheds are named as Grand Reye locally) (2352m). **2hr 50min**

After passing a sign for Path 19 (which is not numbered on the map) cross more rocky ground. The AV1 triangle is not featured on the signpost, but markings can be seen on the rocks ahead along the well-trodden path. Pass the small Lac de Tsan to reach the **Fenêtre de Tsan** (2738m). **4hr 30min** ▸

The views to Lac de Luseney and towards the Comba de Cunéy (the day's final destination) are extensive from this vantage spot.

Descend from the col and then traverse towards the very popular **Lac de Luseney** (2575m). **5hr** Here, the path is marked by arrows painted on the rocks. After crossing some fairly level ground begin to climb up to the final col of the day, **Col de Terray-Terra** (2775m). **5hr 45min**

There is a surprising amount of minor ascent and descent along this section.

The path now enters what feels like a remote combe, which echoes to the sound of eagles soaring from the cliffs above. ◀ After rounding the shoulder of Pointe des Montagnya, traverse the hillside above the alpage of

Reche. There are usually a few patches of old, hard snow to cross along here; fixed ropes aid the traverse and care needs to be taken as it can be slippery. The path from the valley rises to join the AV1 at approximately 2580m. Cross the Torrent de Cunéy via a small bridge, and a final short climb will bring you to **Rifugio Cunéy**. **7hr 05min**

Rifugio Cunéy (tel +39 345 1081551, private, 25 beds, **www.rifugiocuney.it**). This is a reasonably high refuge so the facilities are more basic, but the

The beautiful interior of Santuario di Cunéy

welcome is as warm as elsewhere. Limited (cold) showering is available, and toilets are accessed from outside the main building. A headtorch for night visits is recommended!

The **santuario** is a fascinating church that claims to be the highest in the Aosta Valley at over 2600m. With interesting artwork and lovingly maintained features, it offers a moment's reflection for those seeking a peaceful Alpine corner. It was founded in 1659 to give thanks for the regular supply of water for agriculture in the lower valleys. Numerous developments and extensions to the original chapel have created the structure we see today.

STAGE 11

Rifugio Cunéy to Closé/Oyace/Lexert

Start	Rifugio Cunéy
Distance	12.25km
Total ascent	450m
Total descent	1650m
Grade	2
Time	6hr 15min
Maps	1:50,000 Instituto Geografico Centrale 5: Cervino Matterhorn e Monte Rosa; 1:25,000 Carta dei Sentieri by L'Escursionista editore 6: Valpelline St Barthélemy

This section is predominantly one of descent, but it does include crossing the high Col de Vessona at 2788m, the highest so far with views to match; trekking poles will certainly reduce the impact of the long drop to the valley floor. Descending through 'Avalanche Alley' reminds us of the power of the mountains in the winter. After a night in a hotel in one of the small villages in the valley there will be a spring in the step of many a trekker.

Take the path from the refuge, which passes a small lake before trending south towards the Col du Salvè. **35min** There is a higher path that leaves close to the refuge: this is a protected route (not quite a via ferrata but very exposed).

▸ The AV1 is not mentioned on the sign at the path junction, but it is clearly painted on the rocks at ground level. Take Path 11A to reach **Col de Chaleby** (2683m). **1hr** From the col descend on a reasonably steep, zig-zagging path that eases off before traversing rightwards to a track junction with Path 10. **1hr 20min** Col de Vessona is indicated as being an hour from here.

You are quite likely to spot marmots early in the morning on the way to the col.

The path begins to climb again and the ground turns rockier. Keep following the adequate, painted marks on the ground; the path is well worn and easily followed,

Descending from Col de Chaleby in the early morning sunshine

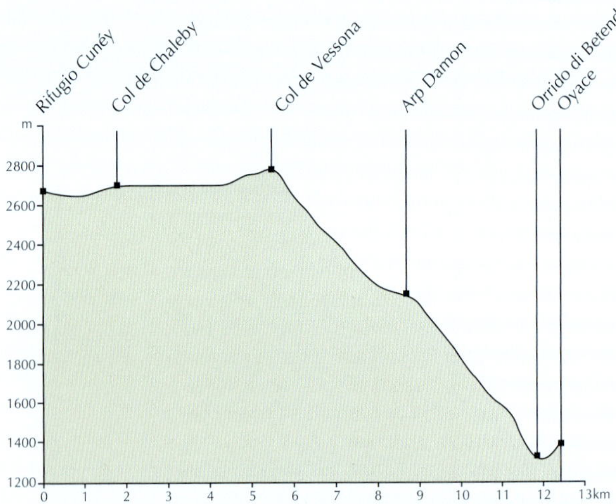

but a keen eye is required to make sure you don't lose it among the boulders. At close to 2700m and after 40min the access path to Bivacco Rosaire et Clermont leaves the path; the Col is about 20min away. ▶ Continue on the path and you will reach the **Col de Vessona** at 2788m. **2hr 20min**

A detour leads to the bivouac hut and its small lake, which makes for a nice resting place; outdoor picnic benches are the finishing touch.

The col offers yet more far-reaching views. The descent requires concentration as it is loose and dusty. Follow the obvious, snaking path. After around 20min, and at around 2300m, the gradient lessens. Continue descending to reach the vegetation line. The path is momentarily difficult to discern as it is somewhat overgrown and sparsely marked. Follow and cross a riverbed to arrive at **Arp Damon** (2206m) (l'Ardamaun on the 1:25,000 map). **3hr 10min**

Keep an eye out for the path descending to the right towards some old farm buildings. Pass these and gain a very good track that descends into the valley below. As the angle eases, leave the tree cover for open ground and the valley floor. You may well encounter avalanche debris in this valley basin, and damaged trees bear evidence of the destructive power of snow. Cross a small **wooden bridge** (1928m) **3hr 55min** and continue along the path to finally descend to a junction in the forest, close to the river where the AV1 is signed right. If you are staying in Oyace, it is possible to follow Path 5 leftwards to Pont de Bagnera and on to **Oyace**. **5hr 15min**

If you are staying in Lexert or Closé, continue down to the right on the AV1 to reach the well-built, high-arched bridge over the **Orrido di Betenda**. **6hr 15min** From here Oyace is signed as 30min away; 20min is more realistic. For Closé or Lexert, follow the Tor des Géants sign rightwards. Climb the path, taking care to follow the yellow arrows. Cross a bridge into a meadow and walk up to the road as it exits Closé. Lexert and the Hotel Valentino are about 10 to 15min to the right; en route you will pass through Places with its old communal bread oven set in the wall. A bus travels up and down the valley. The service is infrequent but, in 2018, buses passed by at 1421 and 1449 and again at 1651.

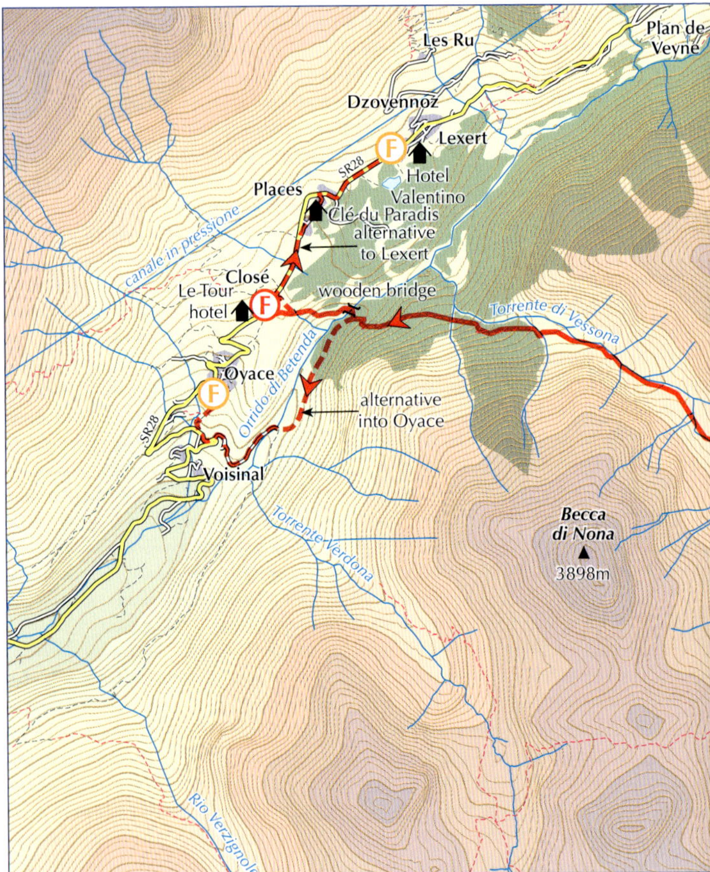

Accommodation: Hotel Valentino, Lexert (12 rooms, tel +39 0165 730901, **www.hotelvalentinobionaz.com**). This pleasant hotel offers basic en-suite rooms, a substantial breakfast and a half-board option (with dinner being served at a nearby restaurant) all at a similar price to a refuge.

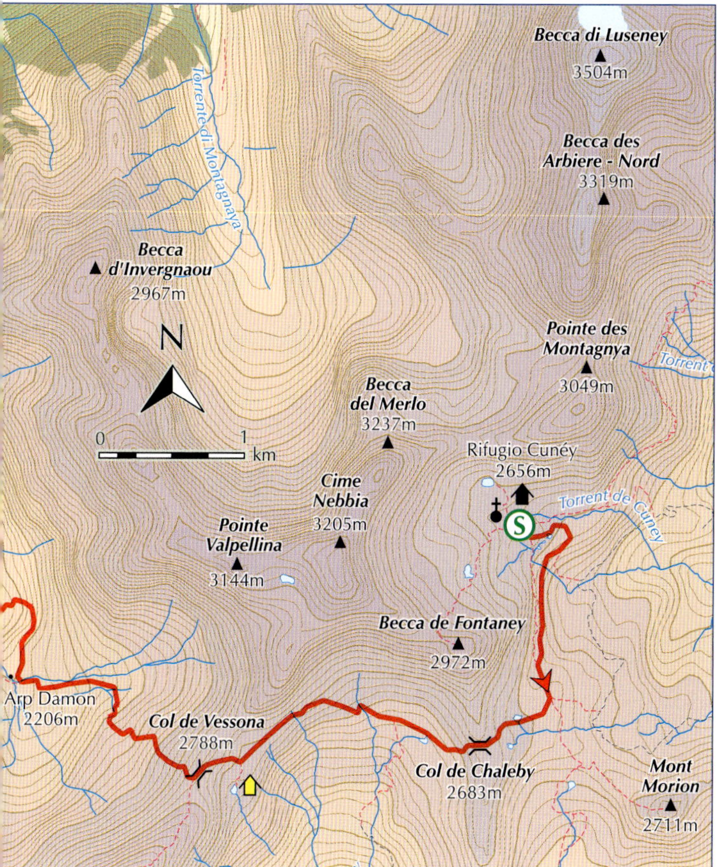

Clé du Paradis B&B (six rooms, tel +39 0165 730016, **www.cleduparadis.it**). This small B&B is a bit of a luxury stopover with its beautifully decorated en-suite rooms. Restaurants can be found nearby in both Lexert and Oyace.

La Tour Hotel, Oyace (double, triple and small *dortoir* accommodation, tel +39 0165 730119 **www.etapelatour.com/it**). Basic en-suite rooms are available at this hotel, as well as a trekkers' *dortoir*. An onsite restaurant offers pizzas and local specialities and a nearby shop sells essential supplies for the coming days.

Facilities: Oyace has a small supermarket and an ATM. Lexert has a 'corner shop' just after the car park on the left and another small shop at the campsite.

Contemplating the valley descent to Oyace.

STAGE 12

Closé/Oyace/Lexert to Ollomont/Rey

Start	Closé/Oyace/Lexert
Distance	11km
Total ascent	1080m
Total descent	1150m
Grade	2
Time	5hr 25min
Maps	1:50,000 Instituto Geografico Centrale 5: Cervino Matterhorn e Monte Rosa; 1:25,000 Carta dei Sentieri by L'Escursionista editore 6: Valpelline St Barthélemy

Crossing the Col de Bresson may well bring lucky trekkers into close contact with eagles cruising the thermals rising from the mountain ridges that soar above. As well as the last views of the Matterhorn, you will see a new vista open up as the latter part of the route begins to come into sight, including a closer view of Mont Blanc. The end of the walk is in sight – albeit several days away.

With a lower alternative route (Stage 12A), and even the possibility of a bus hop, this stage has numerous alternatives. A 'big day' combining this stage with the following short stage can also reduce the total time taken by a day, should time be of the essence.

The hardest part of the day will probably be identifying the correct departure point from the huddle of settlements in Lexert – Closé – Oyace. From Lexert it is necessary to retrace your steps down the valley to reach Closé.

If you are coming from Lexert, a farm track/minor road departs from the main road opposite the farm named 'Condamine' on the L'Escursionista map. Follow this track to the point where the 'official' path joins the road. **5min**

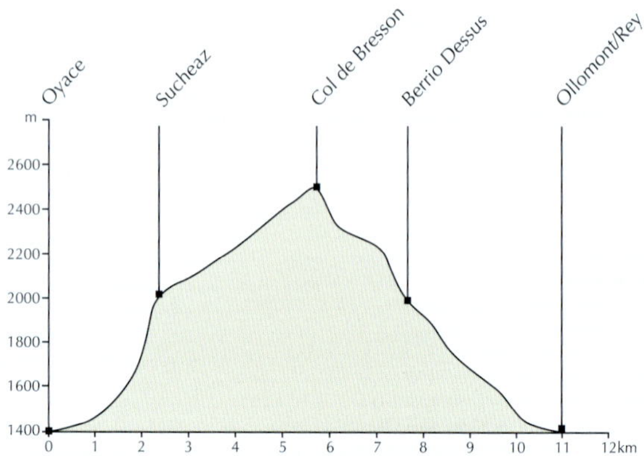

Ascending through the water jets in the fields above Closé (Path 2)

Alternatively, follow the cobbled track that leaves Closé and climbs directly up the slope; this joins the track from Condamine farm. ▶

Painted race arrows are usually evident on the road here, indicating the route (but may be pointing in the opposite direction).

Turn left at this junction (or continue if following the road from the farm) and continue along the road until a sign on the right indicates the AV1 leaves to the right uphill. **10min**

Continue along this path as it initially climbs the hillside before traversing left (west) to cross a gully, which shows evidence of winter avalanches. **25min**

Alternative route

Some mapping shows another option, namely, Path 2. This starts lower in Oyace and climbs through fields on an unmarked path, which may be difficult to follow. It joins the main route just before the gully.

After the gully follow the small but well-formed path that climbs up to **Sucheaz** (1995m). **1hr 15min** Final views of the Matterhorn and also the less well-known Dent d'Hérens can be seen here, and it forms a good place for a first break of the day. Continue following the path through the forest until you reach a small clearing at 2100m and views of Monte Emilius (3559m), a fine, pointed peak across the main valley. When you reach a path junction with Path 3C, and abandoned chalets at Breson l'Arpe (2200m), a sign indicates that the Col de Bresson is 40min away; this will be optimistic for most walkers. **1hr 55min** ▶

It is possible to use Path 3C as an escape route to Valpelline, should you need to make a diversion.

Once you reach the **Col de Bresson**, the views are breathtaking. Grand Combin, Mont Blanc and Monte Emilius are just three of the summits that are clearly visible. The col also makes for a fine lunch stop. **2hr 45min**

The descent from here is via a path that descends alarmingly steep slopes. Fortunately, the path wends a gentler, but longer, route. Soil creep is particularly evident in the numerous natural terraces on this slope. Follow the path taking care at 2450m to ensure that you are still following the AV1. An alternative 'dead end' path leads onto difficult ground. Ollomont and Rey are

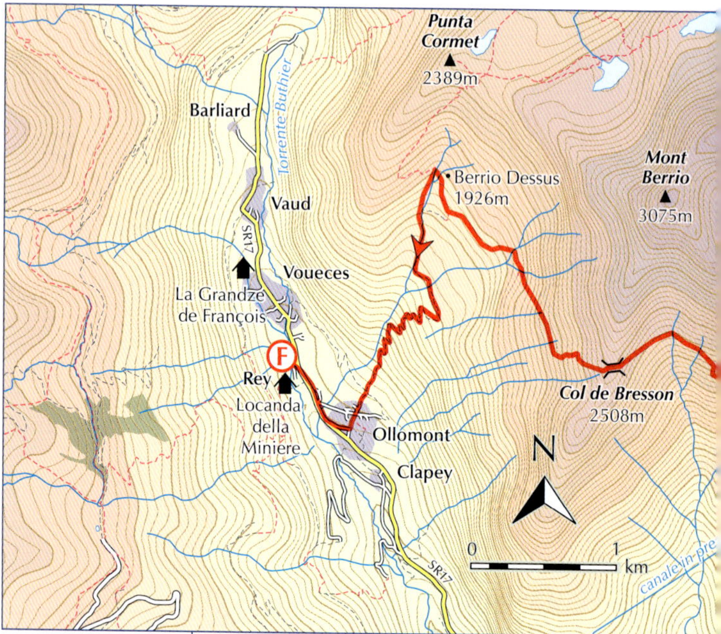

visible far below. At around 2200m the path levels off, which will be a relief for complaining knees! A wooden table and chairs here make for a welcome break. **3hr 20min**

Follow the path as it traverses the hillside, cross a boulder field, which may have avalanche-felled trees to clamber over, and join a farm track **3hr 45min**, which descends towards the farm of **Berrio Dessus** (1926m). **4hr 20min** As you approach the farm, the path is indistinct. Aim for about 100m to the right of the farm, join a track descending left to the actual farm buildings and then take the vehicle track.

Follow the farm access track as it crosses a couple of streams and enters the forest, where it continues its descent to the valley bottom. The track zig-zags down in a series of hairpins.

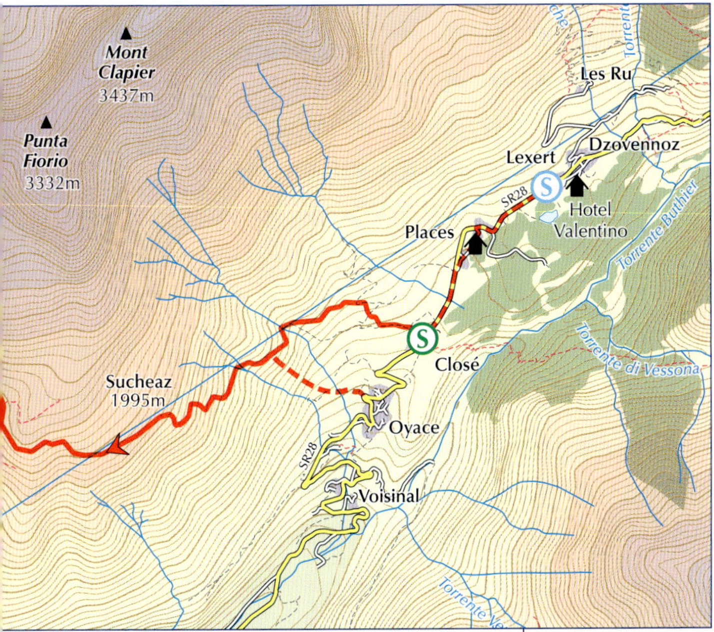

When you reach a small road, cross it and follow the track directly downhill. **5hr 15min** At the second road crossing turn right and follow this road to meet the main valley road. Follow this road up the valley for 150 metres before leaving it on a small road through the car park to reach **Rey**. **5hr 25min**

Accommodation: Locanda della Miniere (five rooms and restaurant, tel +39 0165 1890722, info@locandadelleminiere.it **www.locandadelleminiere.it**). This small, pleasant hotel has good en-suite rooms and a restaurant that serves local specialities and local wines.

About 1km up the valley is another option, **La Grandze de François** (six rooms and restaurant, tel +39 0165 73339, info@lagrandzedefrancois.com

www.lagrandzedefrancois.com). This is another small but well-presented hotel, where local produce and specialities feature heavily on the restaurant's menu. The half-board option is very good value.

Another option is to descend to **Valpelline** from Ollomont, where there are a number of accommodation choices. A bus service leaves Ollomont in the afternoon and returns in the morning. Alternatively, there is a path to the village, Path 2, which takes around an hour in descent.

Facilities: there is a small **shop** in the centre of Ollomont that sells essentials and maps. If this is of interest, then continue down the track instead of turning right at the second crossing.

The chapel in Rey

STAGE 12A

Closé/Oyace/Lexert to Ollomont/Rey: the low route

Start	Closé/Oyace/Lexert
Distance	9.6km
Total ascent	465m
Total descent	485m
Grade	2
Time	2hr 45min
Maps	1:50,000 Instituto Geografico Centrale 5: Cervino Matterhorn e Monte Rosa; 1:25,000 Carta dei Sentieri by L'Escursionista editore 6: Valpelline St Barthélemy; 1:25,000 Carta dei Sentieri by L'Escursionista editore 5: Gran San Bernardo, Valle di Ollomont

The Stage 12 route from the Valpelline valley to Ollomont is quite a challenging day involving significant ascent and descent, the initial descent being across some steep ground. Should the weather be unkind or threatening, this lower route offers a quicker, less-exposed option. There are, however, some awkward moments: the path has no waymarking despite it being a numbered route, and some sections of the path are across reasonably angled slopes. That said, it is no harder than many Lake District paths, and unmarked route navigation is the norm in the UK.

When combined with Stage 13 to Rifugio Champillon, this alternative can be used to make a full day involving around 1400m ascent, and it can also reduce the journey by a day if time is of the essence.

You can use the bus service to reach the village of Valpelline, where you can change for another bus to Ollomont and Rey or follow Path 2 (an old road that takes about an hour and a half). Services run in the early morning and again in the later afternoon.

From the post office in Oyace descend the main road following the pavement to pass the village recreation area and a stream crossing, to reach a hairpin bend that turns

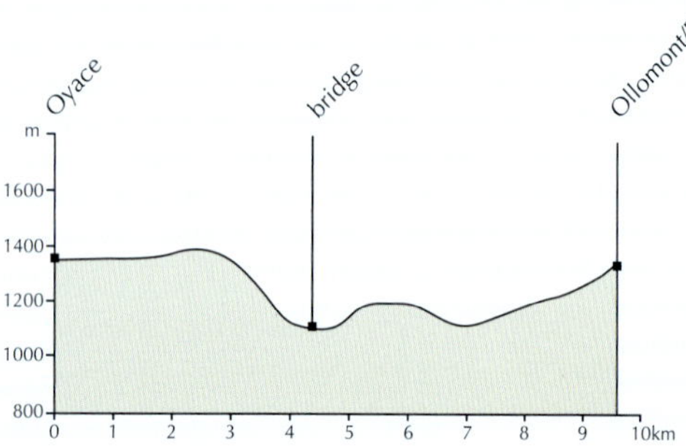
Oyace
bridge
Ollomont/Rey
m
1600
1400
1200
1000
800
0
1
2
3
4
5
6
7
8
9
10km

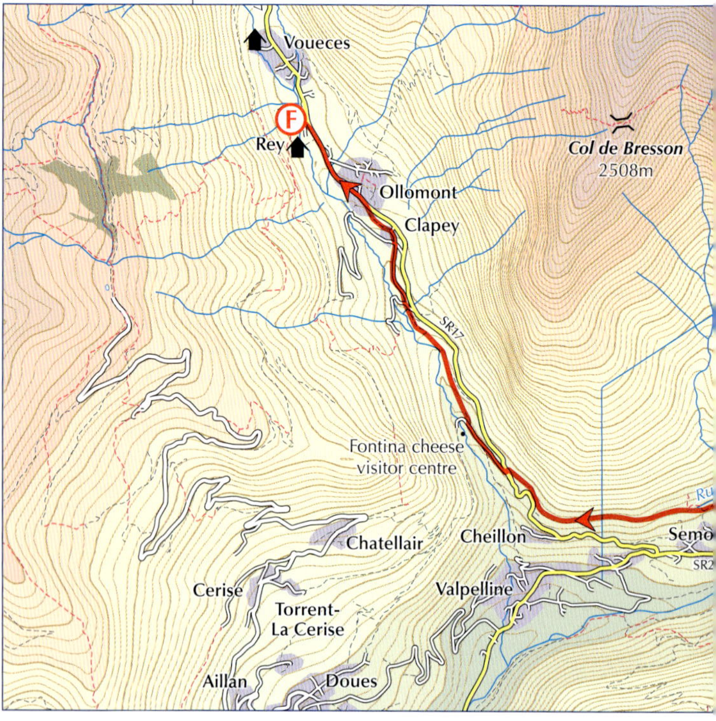
Voueces
F
Rey
Ollomont
Clapey
Col de Bresson
2508m
SR17
Fontina cheese
visitor centre
Chatellair
Cheillon
Cerise
Torrent-
La Cerise
Valpelline
Aillan
Doues

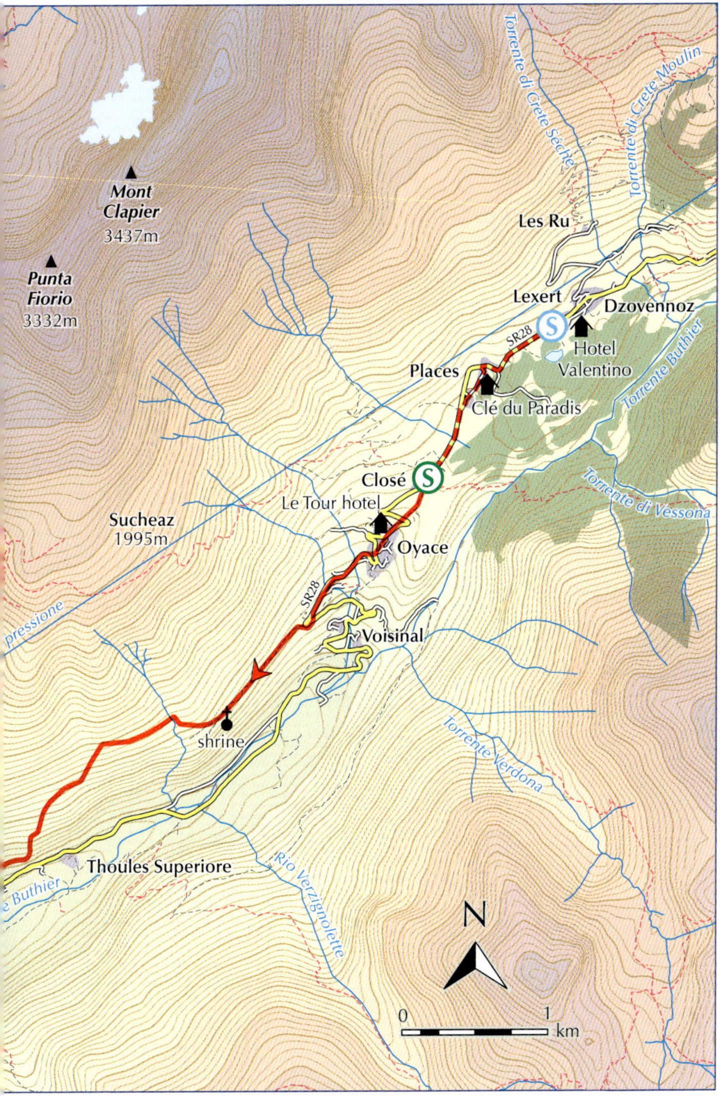
Mont Clapier
3437m
Punta Fiorio
3332m
Torrente di Crete Séche
Torrente di Crete Moulin
Les Ru
Lexert
Dzovennoz
SR28
Hotel Valentino
Places
Clé du Paradis
Torrente Buthier
Closé
Le Tour hotel
Oyace
Torrente di Vessona
Sucheaz
1995m
pressione
SR28
Voisinal
shrine
Torrente Verdona
Thoules Superiore
e Buthier
Rio Verzignolette
N
0
1
km

Looking down on Valpelline

sharp left. Path 1 is signed at the corner of the road but turn the corner and take the track just after, which is easier. Path 1 follows this track for about a kilometre. Take a moment to admire the views both ahead and behind.

Pass a small **shrine**. **15min** Shortly after the chapel take the rising and less-worn track. (The more-worn track services the transmission tower and ceases there.) Climb the track to reach a high point of approximately 1430m and cross a small water course. The path levels off and care needs to be taken to spot the path junction. Take the left, lower fork. **30min** ◂ Follow the path carefully, as it is not as well waymarked as the AV1. At approximately 1200m there is a split in the path; one fork descends steeply downhill to the road while the other bears right. Take the right-hand path, which maintains a level aspect, to reach a wooden footbridge. Cross the bridge over the substantial stream descending from the impressive waterfall. Continue to follow the level path, which is less obvious after this bridge, to reach what appears to be a water treatment building. **1hr 30min**

The path descends quite steeply and, due to the pinecones littering the ground, special care and attention is required in order to avoid a slip.

From this building, climb the track to reach the Ru di-z-Aagne (a covered irrigation channel). Red signs for the ru help. ▶

In late summer the keen forager will probably be able to collect blackberries along the way.

The **ru** were built to manage water supplies before the advent of pumps and hosepipes. They are usually covered small-sized canals with some open sections, reminiscent of Dartmoor leats. As they keep the water flowing at a gentle rate, they make for very pleasant walking on near-level paths, and this is no exception. The section from here to the Ollomont valley is a very pleasant and simple section.

Follow the ru through the dappled shade of the forest to reach the road to Ollomont. **1hr 55min** Follow the road left (downhill) to a junction with a minor road. **2hr** Take this minor road (right), which is signed 'Centro Visita Fontina'. Follow this towards the centre until the road becomes a track at a small chapel. Follow this track as it climbs steadily to reach **Ollomont**. **2hr 45min**

Accommodation: Locanda della Miniere (five rooms and restaurant, tel +39 0165 1890722, info@locandadelleminiere.it **www.locandadelleminiere.it**).

About 1km up the valley is another option, **La Grandze de François** (six rooms and restaurant, tel +39 0165 73339, info@lagrandzedefrancois.com **www.lagrandzedefrancois.com**).

Another option is to descend to **Valpelline** from Ollomont, where there are a number of accommodation choices. A bus service leaves Ollomont in the afternoon and returns in the morning. Alternatively, there is a path to the village, Path 2, which takes around an hour to descend. Further accommodation options are available in Rey, 10min further up the road.

Facilities: a small **shop** in Ollomont (also a café) sells essential supplies, including maps, snacks and sandwiches.

STAGE 13

Ollomont/Rey to Rifugio Champillon

Start	Ollomont/Rey
Distance	4.3km
Total ascent	1040m
Total descent	0m
Grade	2
Time	2hr 40min
Maps	1:50,000 Instituto Geografico Centrale 4: Massiccio del Monte Bianco; 1:25,000 Carta dei Sentieri by L'Escursionista editore 5: Gran San Bernardo, Valle di Ollomont

This is a very short stage that most trekkers will combine with the following stage to make a full day's walk. The official time for this leg is over three hours. This seems very generous, however, and the author has completed the walk in under two and a half hours a number of times. The stage begins with a steady ascent through peaceful forests before you pass a lovely (but locked) church and then ascend summer alpages to a unique refuge.

A veritable feast of berries can be found along the path by the keen forager.

Take the AV1 path, which snakes its way behind the Locanda della Miniere restaurant. Climb the hillside on this path diagonally leftwards. The mixed forest provides good shade from the early sun. ◄ At approximately 1450m join a level path. **10min**

Take the level path leftwards but, almost immediately, begin climbing again. Beware here as the level path is numbered 1 (in a circle), while the AV1 continues to use the more usual AV1 triangular signage.

Follow this path as it climbs to arrive at the old chalet of Prumayes (1621m). **40min** Continue following the path as it doubles back above the chalet and eventually leaves the forest at 1900m. **1hr 30min** Far-reaching views

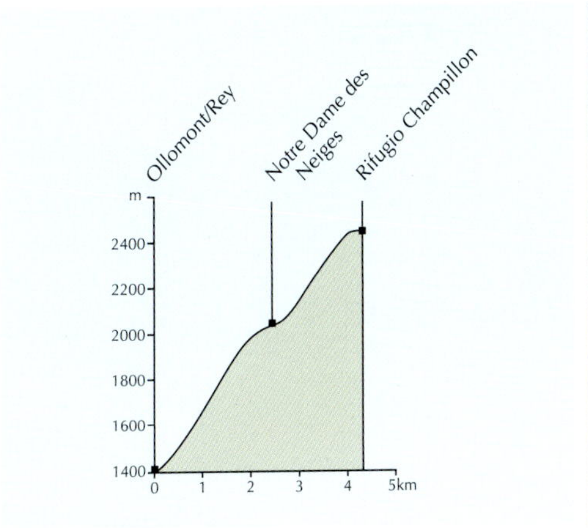
Ollomont/Rey
Notre Dame des Neiges
Rifugio Champillon
m
2400
2200
2000
1800
1600
1400
0
1
2
3
4
5km

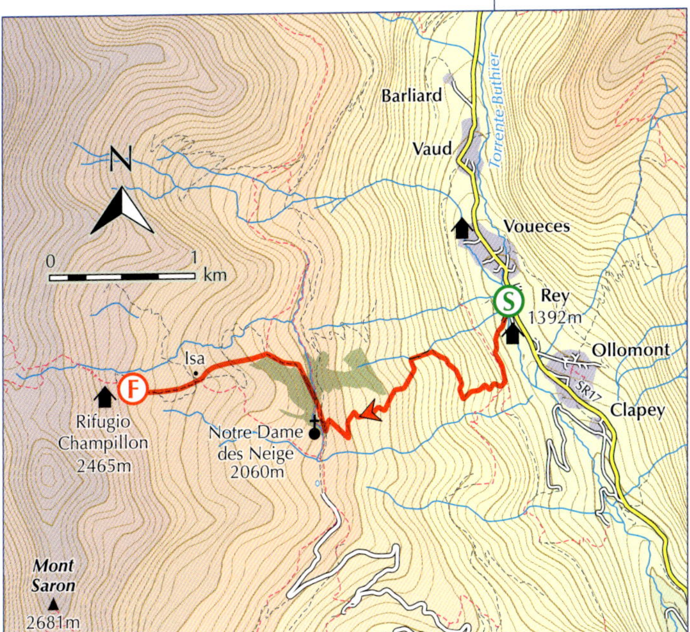
Barliard
Vaud
Torrente Buthier
Voueces
N
0
1
km
S
Rey
1392m
Ollomont
SR17
Clapey
Isa
F
Rifugio
Champillon
2465m
Notre Dame
des Neige
2060m
Mont
Saron
2681m

Climbing to the chapel with Mont Gelé (R) and Grand Combin (L) behind

of Grand Combin and Mont Gelé make for a wonderful backdrop from here.

After leaving the treeline follow the less-distinct path through the meadow towards the church of **Notre Dame des Neiges** visible above. Before reaching the church the path diverts to the farm at Champillon and then returns towards the church. **1hr 50min**

Although the church is locked, a curious look through the barred windows permits a view of the beautifully decorated interior. Follow the obvious vehicle track right (in a northerly direction) but be careful to take the rising track clearly signed to the refuge. Follow this track as it climbs to the farm at Pessinoille. **2hr**

From here take the steeper path that leaves the track. This cuts off a large track bend. Cross the track again and continue climbing the hillside to reach the picturesque farm of Isa (2297m). **2hr 25min** ◂

Local Fontina cheese can be purchased here.

The refuge is close by but remains hidden from view. Follow the vehicle track for about 400 metres until the well-worn path leaves to climb the hillside. Take this path and, before too long, **Rifugio Champillon** comes into sight. **2hr 40min** ▸

You can follow the vehicle track all the way to the refuge should a gentler final approach be required.

Rifugio Champillon (private, 30 beds, tel +39 320 2253348 or +39 339 6359 679, rifugio-champillon@gmail.com **www.rifugio-champillon.it**). With a variety of wellness services on site, including saunas, massage and yoga, Rifugio Champillon, 2465m, built in 2005, is not your typical refuge. It boasts warm showers, some small dormitories and the option for larger groups to stay in a yurt and take meals in the refuge. The local farms supply much of the produce used at the refuge, which prides itself on its environmental credentials.

The eagle-eyed will spot **Fenêtre Durand** in the distance, a pass NE of the refuge that marks the Swiss border. It was used as an escape route to Switzerland by the Italian president, Luigi Einaudi, during the Second World War.

STAGE 14

Rifugio Champillon to Saint-Rhémy-en-Bosses

Start	Rifugio Champillon
Distance	13.4km
Total ascent	420m
Total descent	1300m
Grade	2
Time	4hr 35min
Maps	1:50,000 Instituto Geografico Centrale 4: Massiccio del Monte Bianco; 1:25,000 Carta dei Sentieri by L'Escursionista editore 5: Gran San Bernardo, Valle di Ollomont

After you have made the short climb to the Col Champillon and its far-ranging views, the majority of this stage is a descent to the busy thoroughfare of the Great St Bernard Pass at Saint-Rhémy-en-Bosses. This must be one of the oldest trans-Alpine roads in existence, and it is thrilling to imagine pilgrims from the earliest days of Christianity passing through these villages en route to Rome. The monastery is world famous for providing accommodation to these intrepid travellers; to spend one night in the monastery is an experience many will not want to miss.

It is feasible to reach the Grand San Bernard Monastery and its large dormitories from the refuge should you choose to do so. If this is your aim, a reasonably early start is recommended, as the ascent will take another two and a half hours.

The path from the refuge is obvious and the col is a popular destination in itself. Take the path from the refuge, keeping an eye out for eagles soaring on the morning thermals. As the path levels off, you will pass an intriguing standing stone with a hole through it. Mont Blanc will make a welcome appearance as you reach the summit of the **Col Champillon** (2709m). **50min**

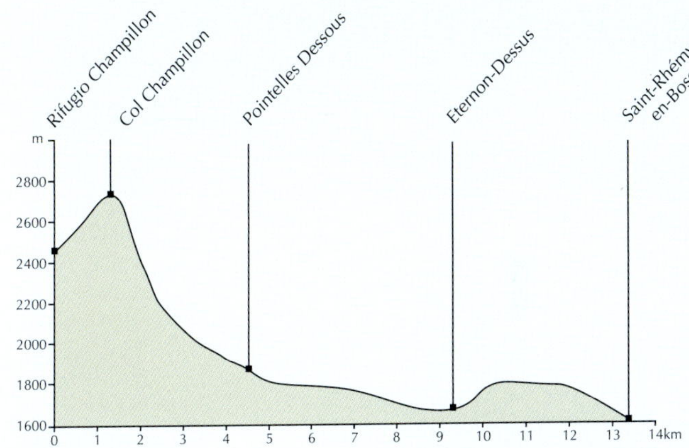

Enjoying the early morning sunshine and far-reaching views

From the col follow the obvious descent path to arrive at some old chalets at 2430m before taking a gentler line to yet more old buildings at Pointelles. **1hr 40min** The path descends steeply here, with a lot of zig-zags easing the gradient.

Continue descending to reach **Pointelles Dessous** (1807m). **2hr 05min** (This is named 'A Pointer Inf 1807m' on the sign at the farm).

Signs for the TDC offer an alternative route choice here. Take the AV1 path, which joins the farm track for about 500 metres. At a hairpin leave the track on a small

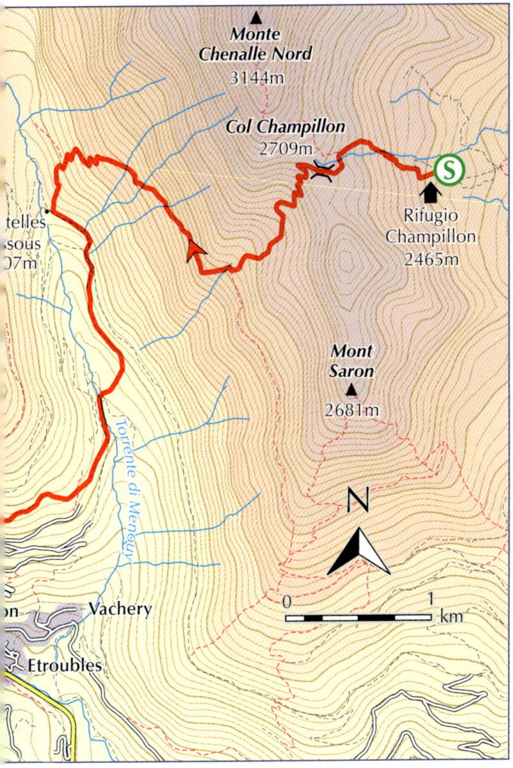

path, effectively heading straight on into some woods. The path undulates on its way to the river. Cross the river on a well-made bridge. **2hr 30min** After a minor climb up from the river take the path that leaves the track (about 300 metres). This path is a lovely old route, and it is easy to imagine people from Roman times wending their way to and from the fields. Pass under some electricity pylons and leave the shade of the trees. ▶ The hamlet of Eternon-Dessus is visible in the middle distance. Drop to the road and follow it into **Eternon-Dessus**. **3hr 10min**

The author has encountered wild boar along this section of the route.

From the chapel follow the signed path uphill along another ancient pathway. After crossing a level path keep climbing and follow AV1 signs into the trees and some welcome shade. When the path joins a good vehicle track **3hr 25min**, turn left and follow this track. This track crosses a stream gully and climbs slightly to 1825m. The path splits here; take the left path, which soon begins to descend. ◂ This track continues until it reaches a road hairpin. **Saint-Rhémy-en-Bosses** is a couple of hundred metres down the road. Care is advised as this is the main road to the Great St Bernard Pass. **4hr 35min**

This is a popular mountain biking route so care may be needed.

The monastery is about two and a half hours from here. See alternative routes 15A and 15B.

Saint-Rhémy-en-Bosses has limited accommodation options; advanced booking is highly recommended. A bus service operates from here to Aosta and to the monastery. **Hotel Suisse** (eight en-suite rooms, tel +39 0165 780901, info@suissehotel.it **www.suissehotel.it**). Hotel Suisse tempts the passer-by to enter into a world of tranquillity; with no TVs present it is something of a retreat. A high-quality restaurant and tasteful Alpine decor add to the ambience.

STAGE 15

Saint-Rhémy-en-Bosses to Rifugio Bonatti

Start	Saint-Rhémy-en-Bosses
Distance	16.5km
Total ascent	1320m
Total descent	900m
Grade	2/3 (Grade 3 over the Col de Malatrà)
Time	6hr 45min
Maps	1:50,000 Instituto Geografico Centrale 4: Massiccio del Monte Bianco; 1:25,000 Carta dei Sentieri by L'Escursionista editore 5: Gran San Bernardo, Valle di Ollomont; 1:25,000 Carta dei Sentieri by L'Escursionista editore 1: Monte Bianco, Courmayeur

Leaving the busy Great St Bernard valley by way of an old road, on which it is easy to imagine farmers and travellers walking since time immemorial, is a magical start to the day. It makes for the perfect start to a reasonably long day travelling across the highest col of the entire route before joining what is probably the most famous trek in the Alps, if not the world, the Tour of Mont Blanc. You will encounter rare Alpine plants along the way as well as some reasonably exposed paths (always protected with ample fixed ropes and metal treadplates). An alternative option is to trek to Rifugio Frassati on this stage and then trek to Courmayeur in a longer final day.

From Hotel Suisse return down the main street to cross the river on the vehicle track bridge following Path 103 (signed St Leonard). **15min** Follow the track leftwards. After 5min the AV1 departs to the right. Take this path, which has multiple signposts for various AV1 destinations, the most important being Rifugio Bonatti. After a short ascent the path resumes a gentle gradient and gives the impression of having been in existence for millennia. Follow the well-maintained track to enter Lavel, where the track becomes a metalled road. Stay on this

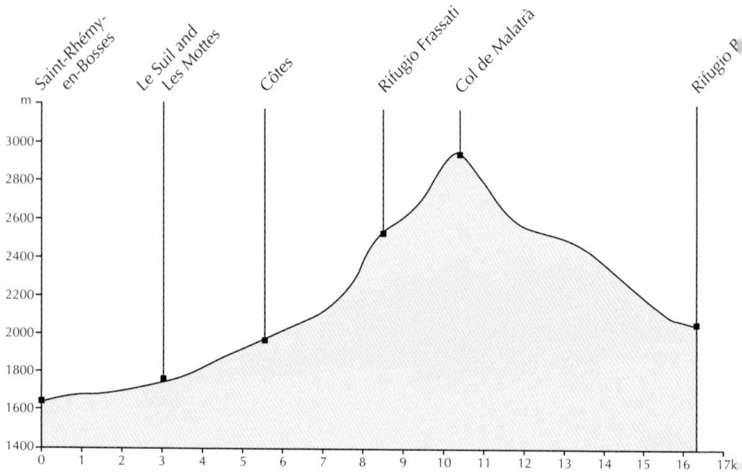

road until it joins a hairpin bend. **25min** At this junction take the lower (left) fork for 100 metres and then take the right-hand fork at the next junction, following signs for Cuchepache and the 'Des Alpes' restaurant. After 200 metres the AV1 is signed to the left. Follow this down through old farm buildings. Keep an eye out for the familiar yellow arrows on building walls along this section. Join another metalled road, which leaves the village, and gently climb up the road to the hamlets of **Le Suil** and **Les Mottes**. **50min** Continue along the road as it passes the ski station car park and then pass underneath the motorway on a forest track. **1hr 05min**

With good vision (or some binoculars) Rifugio Frassati is visible in the mountain bowl high up in the valley ahead.

Continue along the track for 10min until the AV1 is signed at a small path that heads uphill to the right. This path climbs the hillside with ever-improving views as it passes through the abandoned chalets of Merdeux (1950m). **1hr 35min** After climbing for a couple more minutes, the path joins a farm track and is clearly signed AV1. Pass above **Côtes** farmstead and enter the high valley to cross the stream on a small wooden bridge. **2hr 05min** ◂

Climbing towards the small bridge at Moindaz

From the bridge continue for a couple of hundred metres to gain a flatter shoulder. From the shoulder follow the path, which may be indistinct at times, up the valley, eventually joining the vehicle track that serves the dairy farm at Tsa de Merdeux. **3hr 05min** ▸

The AV1 doesn't follow the mapped line here.

Keep following AV1 signs as the path climbs from the dairy up the steep slopes behind. At 2500m **Rifugio Frassati** is signed to the right. **3hr 35min** A detour to the refuge may be tempting for lunch or a coffee; it is a little over 5min away.

The large 'PGF' in white stones on the hillside refers to **Pier Giorgio Frassati**, who was a strong supporter of social justice and a keen mountaineer. Although he was keen to support the poor and those in need, he believed the best way to help lay in social reform. Born into a wealthy family, he gave most of his wealth to the poor. He died at the tender age of 24 from polio. He was beatified in May 1990 by Pope John Paul II.

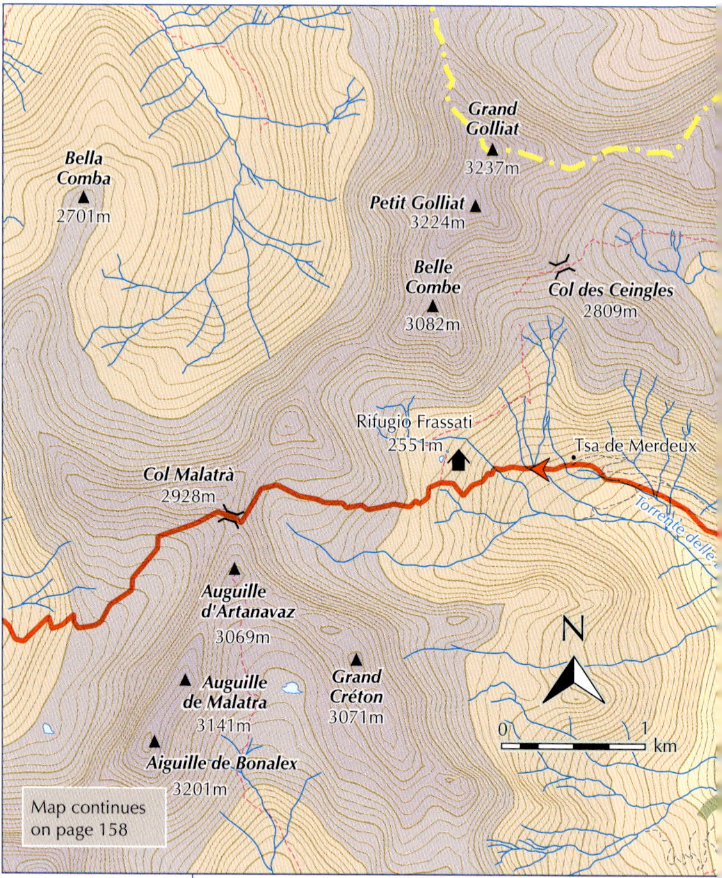

Map continues on page 158

Rifugio Frassati (64 beds, info@rifugiofrassati.it **www.rifugiofrassati.it/en/**). This refuge is operated by the charity Operation Mato Grosso, which raises funds for various missions supporting those in need in Peru, Ecuador, Brazil and Bolivia. The staff are all volunteers and all donations and profits support this work.

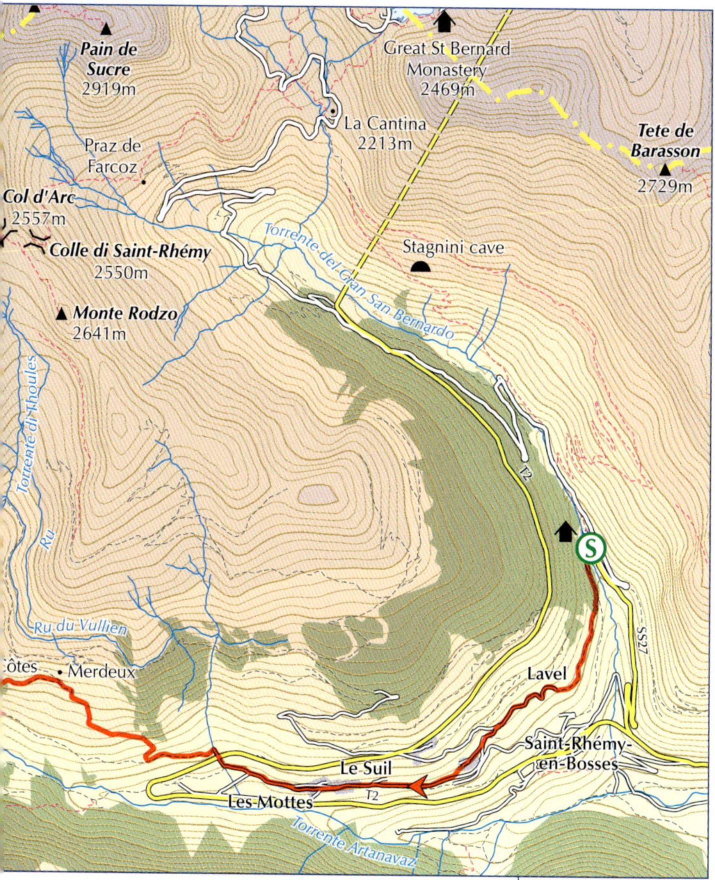

The AV1 is signed to the left and begins the final climb to the Col de Malatrà. Take the well-signed path for the col and the refuge.

This section of the trek climbs through the highest altitudes at which **plant life** grows in any quantity. The range of flowers changes as you gain height

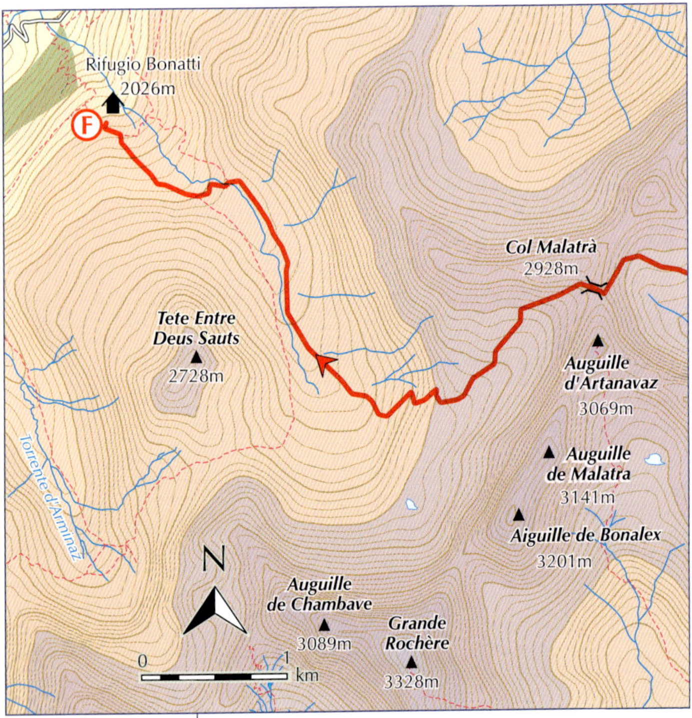

until, among the barren rocks, the rare purple and yellow Alpine toadflax can be spotted.

As the path levels (around 2750m), the final climb of the day can be seen as the trail cuts across the bare scree slopes ahead. **4hr 25min** Cross the scree slope on the well-worn path until it begins to double back on itself. A confident approach is recommended for this traverse. Trekking poles will help with balance as it is of a loose nature in places. This is where the route takes a steeper line and follows fixed rope and metal footsteps bolted onto small rock faces. Using the available aids, follow the line upwards into the thinner air and, after less than

10min of steep ascent, you will gain the **Col de Malatrà** (2928m). **4hr 55min**

The col is the highest point on the AV1 and it is worth taking a moment to celebrate this fact.

▸ The view down the newly acquainted valley is the next stage of the route. Follow the path from the col across the open scree slopes and, early in the season, lingering snow patches. After descending to the vegetation line, follow the path and at around 2600m the path levels off to provide a stunning view of the Mont Blanc massif. **5hr 15min**

After descending a short steeper section of the path, enter a broad river basin and follow the path as it dawdles along beside the river. Pass the high chalets of Giue Damon and cross a small wooden bridge to approach **Rifugio Bonatti** (2026m). Just before the refuge there is a path junction with the world-famous TMB. The refuge is a simple 5min walk from here. **6hr 45min**

Stunning views to be enjoyed on the terrace at Rifugio Bonatti

Rifugio Bonatti (private, 78 beds, tel +39 0165 1855523, **www.rifugiobonatti.it**). Good food, great views and easy access make Rifugio Bonatti a busy hut. It is an important stage post on the Tour of Mont Blanc and an hour's walk from the valley road, so it is always a busy place. Perched across the Val Ferret from the Mont Blanc massif, it offers fantastic views from the terrace.

Walter Bonatti is probably the most famous Italian alpinist: he climbed many first routes on the Mont Blanc range between the 1950s and the 1970s, as well as impressive routes in the greater ranges. He solo-climbed many difficult lines, including the first winter ascent of the North Face of the Matterhorn 100 years after the first ascent. Many of his famous routes on the Grandes Jorasses are visible from the refuge. His first ascent of K2 was surrounded by controversy, and it wasn't until over fifty years later that his version of the ascent was accepted. A prolific author and lover of the mountains, Bonatti continued to campaign for purist, hard climbs. A true mountaineer, the hut is named in his honour.

STAGE 15A

Via Francigena from Saint-Rhémy-en-Bosses to Great St Bernard Monastery

Start	Saint-Rhémy-en-Bosses
Distance	6.1km
Total ascent	780m
Total descent	0m
Grade	2
Time	2hr 40min
Maps	1:50,000 Instituto Geografico Centrale 4: Massiccio del Monte Bianco; 1:25,000 Carta dei Sentieri by L'Escursionista editore 5: Gran San Bernardo, Valle di Ollomont

To walk in the footsteps of pilgrims to probably the most famous monastery in the world is certainly a journey through time. Every step of the way echoes the footsteps of countless travellers between Canterbury, Northern France and Rome. The final approach follows the far older Roman road and passes the remains of Roman temples. The enormous monastery, and home for the night, then comes into view. The equally famous St Bernard dogs are kennelled at the monastery, and a small museum explains the evolution of the hospice and the monastery and provides information about the travellers who crossed the Alps.

The old road to the col is the 'main street' in Saint-Rhémy-en-Bosses, which passes the Hotel Suisse. ▸ Take this road as it heads up and out of the village, passing a small church and statue of the Madonna as it leaves. The predominant signage is for the Via Francigena (Path 103). According to the old saying 'all roads lead to Rome'. It is worth taking a moment here to remember that this road did exactly that.

Note the tops of the lamp posts depicting a pilgrim on his journey to Rome.

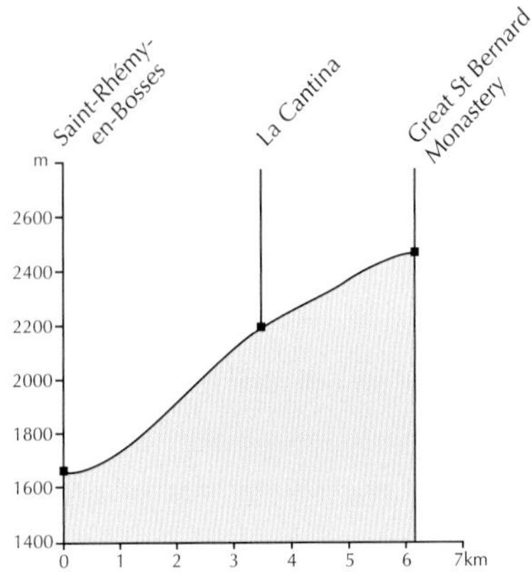

The pilgrim road joins the modern road for about 300 metres before it leaves on the right. Cross the road with care. Path 103 climbs the hillside at a steeper gradient than the road. Be careful not to follow Path 13, which climbs even more steeply. ◂ Path 103 is obviously an old road and displays interesting well-engineered sections as it climbs across the mountainside. A few zig-zags climb the hillside and the path signs change to 13B and the TDC. The pilgrim's road is obvious and continues climbing towards the col. Keep climbing and pass a **cave** with a plaque commemorating the Stagnini gypsies' use of the cave to shelter from snowstorms. **1hr 20min** Continue following the path as it passes well above the Great St Bernard Tunnel entrance until it meets Path 13 (mentioned earlier). **1hr 35min**

Path 13 is an alternative option that climbs more steeply and then enjoys a flatter 'balcony path' before rejoining the Via Francigena at Plan de Raye.

Turn left and follow the path up the valley towards the road. There is a bar/restaurant at **La Cantina** where the path crosses the road. **1hr 45min** Cross the road followed by some pastures to cross the road once more. ◂ Continue following the waymarks across the high pastures towards the impressive galleried road ahead. Before reaching the road, traverse rightwards at

Although another path is marked on the map as taking a much shorter line to the hospice, this is not a feasible route. The TDC/Via Francigena path is far more suitable.

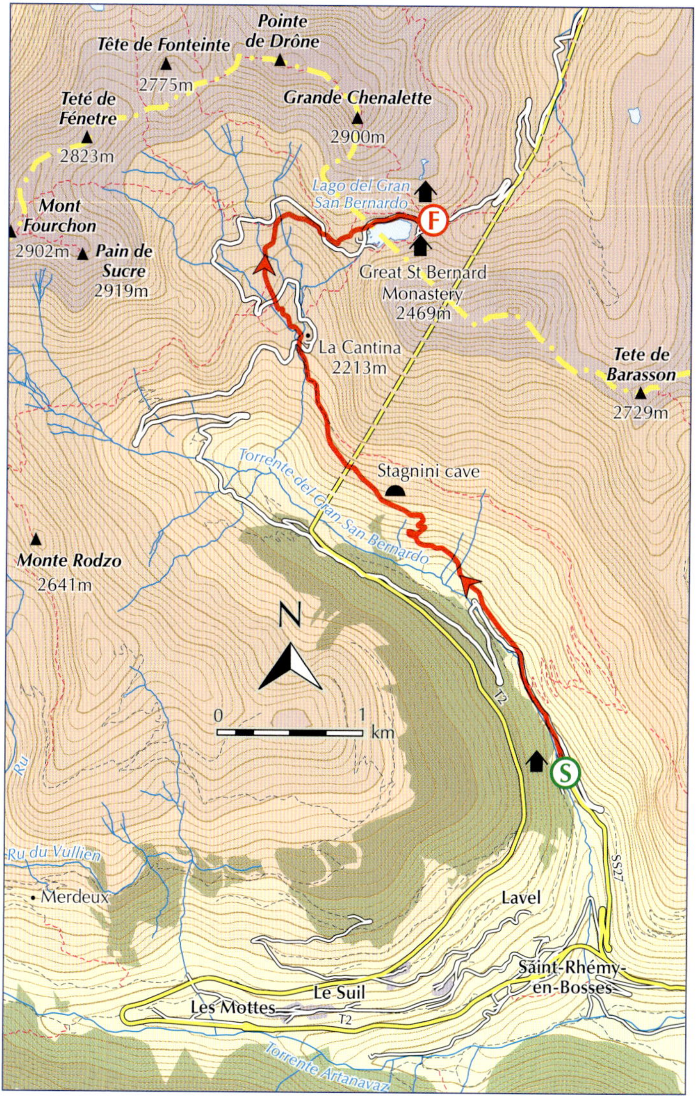
Pointe de Drône
Tête de Fonteinte
2775m
Teté de Fénetre
2823m
Grande Chenalette
2900m
Lago del Gran San Bernardo
F
Mont Fourchon
2902m
Pain de Sucre
2919m
Great St Bernard Monastery
2469m
La Cantina
2213m
Tete de Barasson
2729m
Torrente del Gran San Bernardo
Stagnini cave
Monte Rodzo
2641m
N
0
1
km
T2
S
Ru
Ru du Vullien
SS27
Merdeux
Lavel
Saint-Rhémy-en-Bosses
Le Suil
Les Mottes
T2
Torrente Artanavaz

The monastery comes into view

To pass from Italy into Switzerland you need only cross a stream via a small bridge, as the customs post seems to be permanently closed. However, a passport is still an essential travel document!

a well-signposted path junction to join the road after the gallery section. **2hr 25min** Cross the road carefully as there is a blind bend here and follow the path through a carved-out section to reach the statue of St Bernard. The path drops to join the road, and you will encounter the first of the tourist stalls selling the ubiquitous St Bernard cuddly dogs. Follow the road or, if it is open, the lakeside path to the **Great St Bernard Monastery**. The lakeside path suffers from winter damage (avalanche debris) and may be closed. **2hr 40min** ◂

THE GREAT ST BERNARD PASS AND MONASTERY

Arriving at the Great St Bernard Monastery (2469m) is somewhat bewildering; buses, motorbikes, supercars, cyclists and walkers all vie for position on the road and for tables in the bars and cafés. The actual hospice

The treasury at the monastery

is on the right as you approach; the kennels and museum are to the left along with the hotel entrance. To think that the door has been open to travellers in need of assistance for over 1000 years is truly humbling. In summer there is a flight of 11 steps to the door; in winter ski tourers can ski straight to the door!

The Great St Bernard Monastery, at the high point of the Alpine crossing, is a world-famous building with a fittingly impressive history. Dating back almost a thousand years, the hospice has continued to offer the weary traveller rest and recuperation without charge.

St Bernard founded the monastery in 1049 to help travellers struggling over the high pass between Italy and Switzerland. Many fell foul of the weather; the nearby Combe des Morts gives a clue as to how desperate early or late season crossings could be. Even today it is a dangerous crossing in winter, requiring good mountain skills and a knowledge of the area.

Frequent winter accidents and avalanches meant the monks were, effectively, the world's first mountain rescue team. They developed a breed of dog well suited to searching and recovering those lost or injured; the St Bernard was born.

The dogs are no longer used as routine search and rescue dogs; helicopters and smaller, more agile breeds fulfil this role. However, the dogs remain a strong aspect of life at the col, and the kennels welcome visitors each day.

Probably the most famous traveller to cross the col is Napoleon, who passed through with 40,000 troops. Although in reality he crossed astride a mule, the iconic painting by Jacques Louis David depicts Napoleon mounted on a rearing stallion pointing onwards. Napoleon issued the nearby village of Bourg-Saint-Pierre a promissory note to pay for food and supplies as part of this crossing. The debt remained unpaid until the French President, François Mitterand, visited in 1983 and settled the outstanding bill!

Staying at the monastery

The monastery has been welcoming travellers for over a millennium. In recent times a privately owned hotel, the Auberge de L'Hospice, has opened, offering more luxurious accommodation within the monastery complex. The monastery itself offers traditional *dortoir* accommodation and some private rooms on a half-board basis. Even though there are over 150 beds, it is still advisable to book in advance. Payment can be made in Swiss Francs or by credit card. **Hospice:** tel +41 27 787 12 36, hospice@gsbernard.com **www.gsbernard.com**. **Hotel:** tel +41 27 7871153, info@aubergehospice.ch **www.aubergehospice.ch**. The hotel has 30 en-suite rooms, all of which are of a good standard. A small restaurant on site offers a range of local products, including a fondue made with Trappist beer, the author's favourite! A small gift shop, a museum and the kennels all offer the early visitor plenty to keep him or her occupied.

The entrance to the monastery in the winter

STAGE 15B

Great St Bernard Monastery to Rifugio Bonatti

Start	Great St Bernard Monastery
Distance	15.75km
Total ascent	1150m
Total descent	1510m
Grade	2
Time	6hr 50min
Maps	1:50,000 Instituto Geografico Centrale 4: Massiccio del Monte Bianco; 1:25,000 Carta dei Sentieri by L'Escursionista editore 5: Gran San Bernardo, Valle di Ollomont; 1:25,000 Carta dei Sentieri by L'Escursionista editore 1: Monte Bianco, Courmayeur

Crossing three cols makes this a long day, particularly as the last col is also the highest point on the AV1 route at over 2900m. With such high places come new challenges; the surroundings are rocky and the plants reflect this harsh, high environment. The views are superlative and Mont Blanc becomes the backdrop for the final night in the mountains, a fitting climax to a stunning journey. Should Rifugio Bonatti be fully booked, it is also possible to stay at Rifugio Frassati, less than 4hr from the monastery and then walk to Courmayeur from there.

From the hospice take the road back into Italy and retrace your route past the St Bernard statue and cross the road before the galleries to a path junction. **20min**

Follow Path 103 towards La Cantina but, at the lower end of a long, low wall take the path rightwards to cross the road (Path 12A) at a rough car park area. Keep following Path 12A as it gently climbs from the road. Round a shoulder and continue following the path as it drops gently to cross a stream. ▸ After crossing the stream ascend to pass above the farm of **Praz de Farcoz**. **1hr** Follow the path, which is indistinct at times as it is overgrown

This part of the path is subject to more natural erosion and calls for additional care.

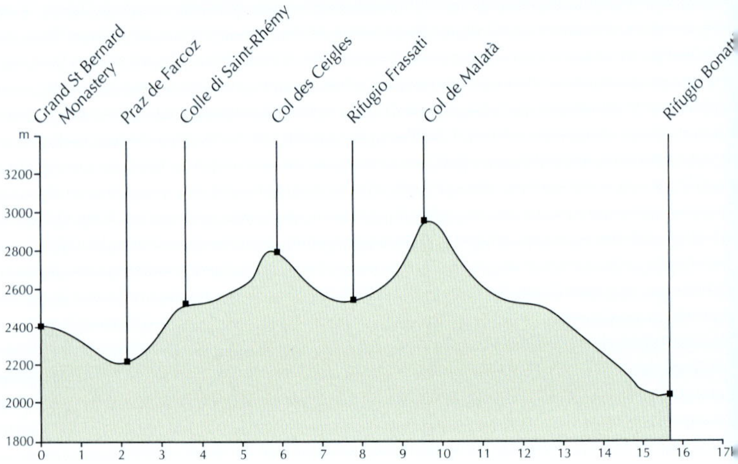

in places, to another stream crossing and the beginning of a climb up a long open valley. The path meanders up

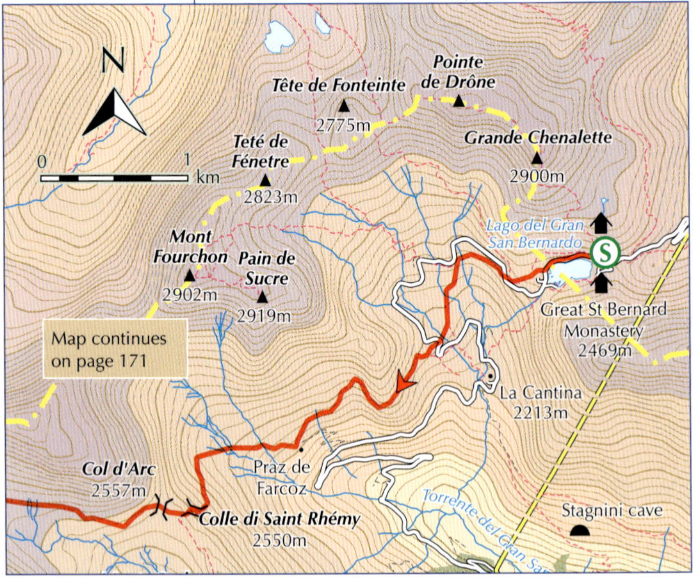

this slope past a large, distinctive rock that has Path 12 and 12A waymarkers painted on it. Follow the path as it zig-zags up the final few metres, and you will eventually reach the **Colle di Saint-Rhémy** (2550m) and its sister **Col d'Arc** (2557m). **2hr**

There is a stunning view from the col, and a very useful orientation table helps you to identify the surrounding summits. Take the path to the right and begin a steep descent, which soon eases into a gentler downwards path to the isolated and flower-strewn Comba des Thoules. ▸ Follow Path 12A and climb towards the Col des Ceingles at the head of the visible valley. This is a delightful walk with blankets of vetch and moss campion forming bright-yellow and deep-pink carpets along the way. At around 2650m

The double cols of this summit area could be confusing in poor visibility.

Descending towards Rifugio Frassati from the Col des Ceingles

you will reach the limit of vegetation growth, and the terrain turns rocky. You may well see chamois and ibex in the distance in this unfrequented valley. The loose nature of the scree is unwelcome but is never too onerous. Arrive at **Col des Ceingles** (2809m). **2hr 50min**

Once more, the initial descent is quite steep and feels mountainous. After descending this short steep slope, cross an unnamed col at 2772m and follow the path down the open slopes. ◂

You may encounter some old snow patches along this section of the route, but occasional upright marker stones help if the path becomes indistinct.

Where the path levels off, follow the upright stones to descend a lateral moraine and then bear rightwards on the path to cross two small streams before arriving at **Rifugio Frassati** (2551m). **3hr 40min**

The large 'PGF' in white stones on the hillside refers to **Pier Giorgio Frassati**, who was a strong supporter

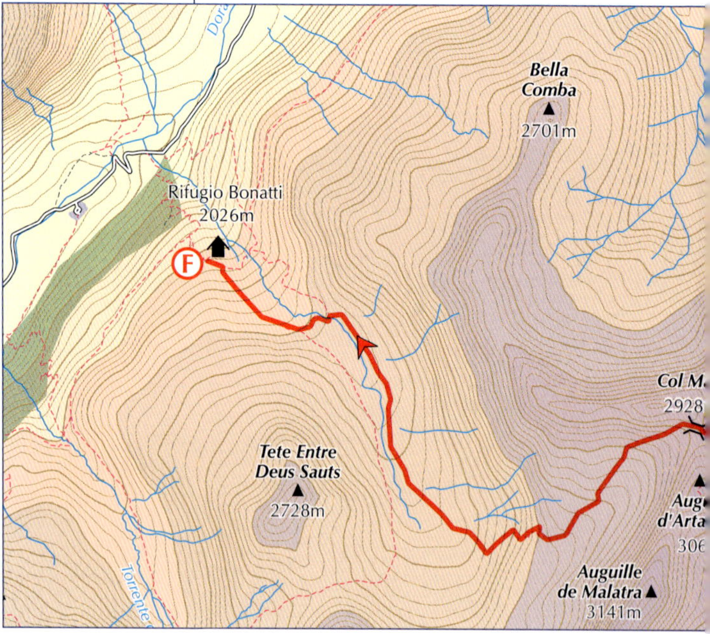

of social justice and a keen mountaineer. Although he was keen to support the poor and those in need, he believed the best way to help lay in social reform. Born into a wealthy family, he gave most of his wealth to the poor. He died at the tender age of 24 from polio. He was beatified in May 1990 by Pope John Paul II.

Rifugio Frassati (64 beds, info@rifugiofrassati.it **www.rifugiofrassati.it/en/**).This refuge is operated by the charity Operation Mato Grosso, which raises funds for various missions supporting those in need in Peru, Ecuador, Brazil and Bolivia. The staff are all volunteers and all donations and profits support this work.

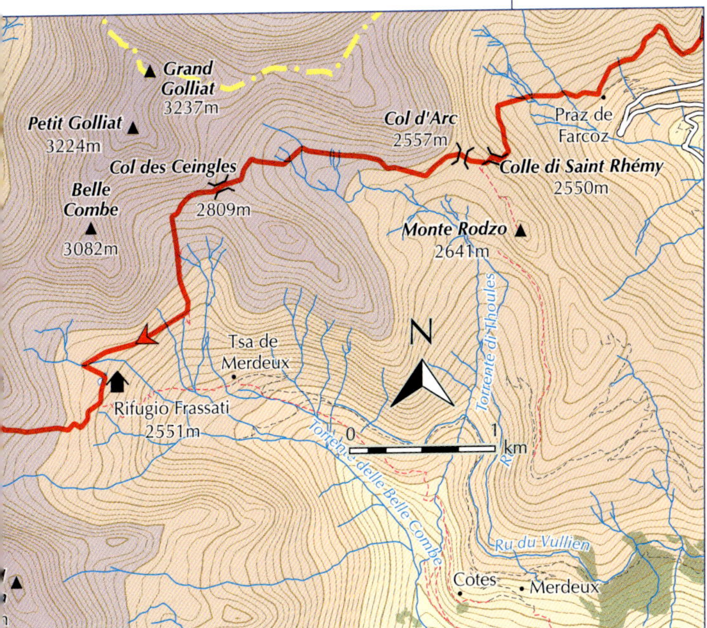

Rifugio Frassati

The next objective is the Col de Malatrà and then onwards to Rifugio Bonatti. Take the well-signed path for the col and the refuge.

> This section of the trek climbs through the highest altitudes at which **plant life** grows in any quantity. The range of flowers changes as you gain height until, among the barren rocks the rare purple and yellow Alpine toadflax can be spotted.

As the path levels (around 2750m), the final climb of the day can be seen as the trail cuts across the bare scree slopes ahead. **4hr 30min** Cross the scree slope on the well-worn path until it begins to double back on itself. A confident approach is recommended for this traverse. Trekking poles will help with balance as it is of a loose nature in places. This is where the route takes a steeper line and follows fixed rope and metal footsteps bolted onto small rock faces. Using the available aids, follow the line upwards into the thinner air and, after less than 10min of steep ascent, you will gain the **Col de Malatrà** (2928m). **5hr**

▸ The view down the newly acquainted valley is the next stage of the route. Follow the path from the col across the open scree slopes and, early in the season, lingering snow patches. After descending to the vegetation line, follow the path and at around 2600m the path levels off to provide a stunning view of the Mont Blanc massif. **5hr 20min**

The col is the highest point on the AV1 and it is worth taking a moment to celebrate this fact.

After descending a short steeper section of the path, enter a broad river basin and follow the path as it dawdles along beside the river. Pass the high chalets of Giue Damon and cross a small wooden bridge to approach **Rifugio Bonatti**. Just before the refuge there is a path junction with the world-famous TMB. The refuge is a simple 5min walk from here. **6hr 50min**

Rifugio Bonatti (private, 78 beds, tel +39 0165 1855523, **www.rifugiobonatti.it**). Good food, great views and easy access make Rifugio Bonatti a busy hut. It is an important stage post on the Tour of Mont Blanc and an hour's walk from the valley road, so it is always a busy place. Perched across the Val Ferret from the Mont Blanc massif, it offers fantastic views from the terrace.

Walter Bonatti is probably the most famous Italian alpinist: he climbed many first routes on the Mont Blanc range between the 1950s and the 1970s, as well as impressive routes in the greater ranges. He sol o-climbed many difficult lines, including the first winter ascent of the North Face of the Matterhorn 100 years after the first ascent. Many of his famous routes on the Grandes Jorasses are visible from the refuge. His first ascent of K2 was surrounded by controversy, and it wasn't until over fifty years later that his version of the ascent was accepted. A prolific author and lover of the mountains, Bonatti continued to campaign for purist, hard climbs. A true mountaineer, the hut is named in his honour.

STAGE 16

Rifugio Bonatti to Courmayeur

Start	Rifugio Bonatti
Distance	11.2km
Total ascent	150m
Total descent	950m
Grade	2
Time	3hr 55min
Maps	1:50,000 Instituto Geografico Centrale 4: Massiccio del Monte Bianco; 1:25,000 Carta dei Sentieri by L'Escursionista editore 1: Monte Bianco, Courmayeur

With an early start Mont Blanc will, hopefully, present itself clear of mist and cloud for the final 'balcony' walk and descent to the mountain town of Courmayeur.

The final stage doesn't fail to impress. Sharing the way with the world-famous TMB means there'll be plenty of traffic, but even so it will be perfectly possible to find a quiet spot for a break and a little time for reflection on your journey over the previous couple of weeks. The hustle and bustle of even a small town will come as something of a shock after the comparative peace and quiet of the mountains. At the end of the day you will have richly earned a celebration. The biggest challenge, however, will be deciding what to order from any of the many quality restaurants in Courmayeur.

From the refuge descend leftwards towards the enormous bulk of Mont Blanc and breathtaking views. The path levels to pass above the alpage of **Secheron** before it gently climbs to a corner and enters the side valley of Combe d'Arminaz. Ignore the vague path that descends below and follow the main path to join Path 29. **40min**

Cross a wooden **bridge** and climb out of the combe to enter a section that is well worn and which suffers from erosion and mud, even in high summer. After you pass the junction with Path 30, you will encounter

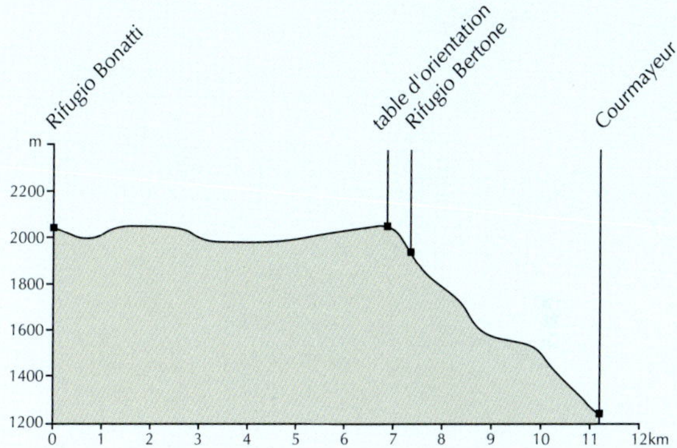

a small pond that offers wonderful reflections of Mont Blanc. **1hr 30min** ▸

After passing Alpe Leuchey, 1938m, gently climb to arrive at a *table d'orientation* at 2055m and a path junction. **2hr 15min** From here it is downhill all the way to Courmayeur!

Descend the well-signed path to pass **Rifugio Bertone** (1977m). **2hr 25min** Descend a series of zigzags into the Val Sapin, passing a military memorial on the way, to join a track that can be followed, although the AV1 cuts some of the corners.

You can take Path 30 down to Meyencet and the road on which a bus stop is located.

The memorial commemorates the **Aosta Battalion**, an elite group of soldiers with specific mountain skills. During the First World War the battalion was awarded the MOVM, Gold Medal of Military Valour, in recognition of their actions on Monte Solarolo in which 23 of the 25 officers and 773 of the 800 troops were injured or killed repelling the invading Austrian forces in the Veneto region of Italy.

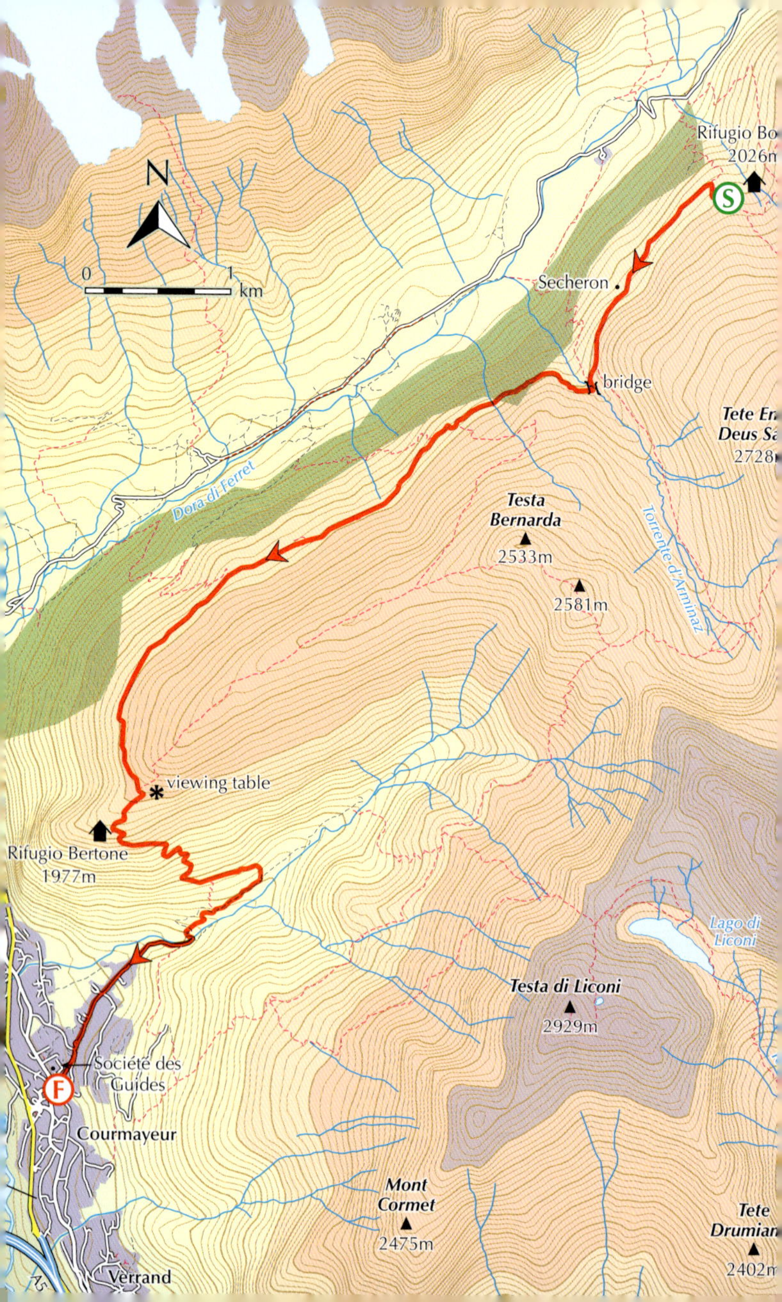

N
0
1
km
Rifugio Bo
2026m
S
Secheron
bridge
Tete En
Deus Sa
2728
Dora di Ferret
Testa
Bernarda
2533m
2581m
Torrente d'Arminaz
viewing table
Rifugio Bertone
1977m
Lago di
Liconi
Testa di Liconi
2929m
F
Société des
Guides
Courmayeur
Mont
Cormet
2475m
Tete
Drumian
2402m
Verrand

The military memorial to the Aosta Battalion who served in the First World War

The track gradually becomes a road. Keep descending, passing a memorial to the mountain guides of Courmayeur, before suddenly popping out into the heart of the town of **Courmayeur** at the Société des Guides. **3hr 55min**

There is no official finish to the AV1 but the small square makes as good a finish point to the trek as any other, and the plentiful bars and cafés will be able to offer suitable celebrations. With a reasonably early start you will be able to enjoy a celebratory lunch in the heart of Courmayeur, pondering the sights and experiences of the previous two weeks or so.

COURMAYEUR

The AV1 emerges from the mountains at Piazza Abbé Henry and delivers the triumphant AV1 finisher into the very heart of the town. The short final stage should allow for a perfect lunchtime finish in the centre of the town. Turn left or right and delightful cafés, restaurants and shops line the street, which is closed to traffic.

Courmayeur retains a feeling of authenticity. Sitting beneath Mont Blanc and surrounded by soaring peaks, it is a true mountain town. The main street, Via Roma, is a bustling thoroughfare that harks back to previous centuries. Thanks to modern pedestrianisation, it is a perfect place to wander and enjoy a relaxing drink to celebrate the conclusion of the AV1.

The town has a good range of cafés from which to sit and watch the world go by; without doubt there will be backpackers coming and going. Courmayeur is almost halfway around the TMB and caters superbly for the trekker. Countless shops offer souvenirs and typical Savoyard products, as well as tempting outdoor purchases.

A small museum called the Società Guide Alpine di Courmayeur offers an insight into the world of mountaineering and makes for a pleasant hour or so in the afternoon. The bus station lower down in the town features a pair of super-sized crampons (the world's largest ice axe is claimed to be in L'Argentière-la-Bessée in France). The famous Skyway Monte Bianco, a short bus ride away, can take you in a rotating gondola to a truly awe-inspiring viewpoint and a scene from the recent Bond film, *Spectre*.

With plenty to see, do and eat, an afternoon in Courmayeur is the perfect icing on this particular Alpine cake!

The bus station and tourist information office are located at the lower part of town, pretty much straight downhill from the Société des Guides.

APPENDIX A

Two-week schedule

	Stage	Time	Distance	Ascent	Descent
A two-week variation					
1	Donnas to Sassa (Etoile du Berger)	5hr 20min	9.8km	1550m	500m
2	Sassa to Rifugio Barma (via Col Portola)	6hr	10.4km	1310m	615m
3	Rifugio Barma to La Gruba (Niel)	7hr 10min	13.7km	900m	1400m
4	La Gruba (Niel) to Gressoney-Saint-Jean	6hr 45min	16.25km	900m	1140m
5	Gressoney-Saint-Jean to Vieux Crest	5hr 50min	11.1km	1400m	900m
6	Vieux Crest to Rifugio Grand Tournalin	4hr	9.5km	1020m	450m
7	Rifugio Grand Tournalin to Rifugio Barmasse	6hr 30min	11.8km	1000m	1300m
8	Rifugio Barmasse to Rifugio Cunéy	7hr 10min	14.2km	1200m	650m
9	Rifugio Cunéy to Oyace	6hr	12.25km	450m	1650m
10	Oyace to Ollomont/Rey	5hr 25min	11km	1080m	1150m
11	Ollomont/Rey to Saint-Rhémy-en-Bosses	7hr 20min	17.7km	1460m	1300m
12	Saint-Rhémy-en-Bosses to Rifugio Bonatti	6hr 40min	16.5km	1320m	900m
13	Rifugio Bonatti to Courmayeur	3hr 55min	11.2km	150m	950m

APPENDIX B

Useful contacts

Transport

Trek-bus
tel + 39 0166 940986

SAVDA (buses)
www.savda.it

SVAP (buses)
www.svap.it

Tourist offices

www.lovevda.it

Breuil-Cervinia
tel +39 0166 949136
cervinia@turismo.vda.it

Gressoney-Saint-Jean
tel +39 0125 355185
gressoneysaintjean@turismo.vda.it

Aosta
tel +39 0165 236627
aosta@turismo.vda.it

Trek accommodation and mountain refuges

Etoile du Berger (hotel)
twin and double rooms
tel +39 340 5206774
www.letoileduberger.it

Rifugio Coda
CAI, sleeps 51
tel +39 152 562405
rifugiocoda@libero.it

Rifugio Barma
independent, sleeps 54
tel +39 331 1087009
rifugiobarma@gmail.com
www.rifugiobarma.it

Rifugio della Vecchia
private, 20 beds
tel +39 015 885 3232
valeria@rifugiolagodellavecchia.com

Rifugio Rivetti
CAI, sleeps 53
tel +39 15 2476141
sandrozoia@libero.it

La Gruba Hotel
16 beds
tel +39 340 8270110
www.lagruba.com

For **Gressoney-Saint-Jean** tourist information
tel +39 0125 355185
gressoneysaintjean@turismo.vda.it

Rifugio Alpenzu
private, 20 beds
tel +39 338 2562229
info@rifugioalpenzu.it
www.rifugioalpenzu.it

Rifugio Vieux Crest
private, 36 beds
tel +39 0125 307983
info@refugevieuxcrest.com
www.lavarets.it/rifugio-alpino-vieux-crest

Rifugio Gran Tournalin
private, 45 beds
tel +39 0125 307003
www.rifugiograndtournalin.com

Rifugio Barmasse
private, sleeps 25
tel +39 345 1081551
www.rifugiocuney.it/it/il-rifugio-barmasse

Rifugio Cunéy
private, 25 beds
tel +39 345 1081551
www.rifugiocuney.it

Hotel Valentino, Lexert
12 rooms, half board available
tel +39 0165 730901
www.hotelvalentinobionaz.com

Clé du Paradis B&B
6 rooms, restaurants in nearby Lexert
tel +39 0165 730016
www.cleduparadis.it

La Tour Hotel, Oyace
dortoir accommodation option, restaurant on site
tel +39 0165 730119
www.etapelatour.com/it

Locanda della Miniere (hotel), Ollomont
5 rooms and restaurant
tel +39 0165 1890722
info@locandadelleminiere.it
www.locandadelleminiere.it

Rifugio Champillon
private, 30 beds
tel +39 320 2253348 or +39 339 6359 679
rifugiochampillon@gmail.com
www.rifugio-champillon.it

Hotel Suisse, Saint-Rhémy-en-Bosses
tel +39 0165 780901
info@suissehotel.it
www.suissehotel.it

Great St Bernard Hospice
tel +41 27 787 12 36
hospice@gsbernard.com
www.gsbernard.com

Great St Bernard Hotel
tel +41 27 787 11 53
info@aubergehospice.ch
www.aubergehospice.ch

Rifugio Frassati
private (charitable trust), 64 beds
tel + 39 331 943 8054
info@rifugiofrassati.it
www.rifugiofrassati.it/en/

Rifugio Bonatti
private, 78 beds
tel +39 0165 1855523
www.rifugiobonatti.it

Links to accommodation throughout the Aosta Valley can be found at www.aosta-valley.co.uk.

Mapping
Swiss Topo – includes app (from Gressoney onwards)
www.swisstopo.ch

Weather
YR – includes app
www.yr.no/?spr=eng

Miscellaneous
Alpine Flowers by Gillian Price (Cicerone).

'The world of Alpine flowersie' – app (identifies Alpine flowers)

APPENDIX C

Useful phrases

As part of the old Kingdom of Savoy, the Aosta Valley is a multilingual area. French is often spoken as capably as Italian. English tends to be spoken less frequently (more so in the tourist hotspots). A well-intentioned attempt in either Italian or French will be welcomed.

Pleasantries and manners

English	Italian	French
thank you	*grazie*	*merci*
please	*per favore*	*s'il vous plaît*
hello, good day	*buon giorno*	*bonjour*
good evening/goodnight	*buona sera*	*bonsoir*
goodbye	*arrivederci*	*au revoir*
less formal greeting 'hi'	*salve*	*salut*

Navigation/route-finding

English	Italian	French
left	*sinistra*	*gauche*
right	*destra*	*droit*
ahead	*avanti*	*tout droit*
map	*carta*	*carte*
compass	*bussola*	*boussole*
guidebook	*guida*	*guide*
route	*itinerario*	*parcours*
north	*nord*	*nord*
south	*sud*	*sud*
east	*est*	*est*
west	*ovest*	*ouest*
stage/leg (in a walk)	*tappe*	*étape*

English	Italian	French
path (a footpath)	*sentiero*	*sentier*
track (off-road vehicle track)	*carreggiabile*	*chemin*
road	*strada*	*route*
ridge	*creta*	*crête*
pass	*colle*	*col*
glacier	*glacier*	*glacier*
summit	*vetta*	*sommet*
tarn, small lake	*lac/lago*	*lac*
junction	*incrocio*	*jonction*
stream	*corrente*	*ruisseau*
river	*fiume*	*rivière*
wood	*bosco*	*bois*
rock	*rocce*	*rocher*
dam	*diga*	*barrage*
bridge	*ponte*	*pont*

Accommodation

English	Italian	French
mountain hut	*rifugio*	*refuge*
half board	*mezza pensione*	*demi-pension*
dormitory	*dormitorio*	*dortoir*
tent	*tenda*	*tente*
campsite	*area di campeggio*	*camping*

Numbers

English	Italian	French
zero	*zero*	*zéro*
one	*uno*	*un*
two	*due*	*deux*
three	*tre*	*trois*
four	*quattro*	*quatre*

English	Italian	French
five	*cinque*	*cinq*
six	*sei*	*six*
seven	*sette*	*sept*
eight	*otto*	*huit*
nine	*nove*	*neuf*
ten	*diece*	*dix*
eleven	*undici*	*onze*
twelve	*dodici*	*douze*
thirteen	*tredici*	*treize*
fourteen	*quattrodici*	*quatorze*
fifteen	*quidici*	*quinze*
sixteen	*sedici*	*seize*
seventeen	*diciassette*	*dix-sept*
eighteen	*diciotto*	*dix-huit*
nineteen	*diciannove*	*dix-neuf*
twenty	*venti*	*vingt*
thirty	*trenta*	*trente*
forty	*quaranta*	*quarante*
fifty	*cinquantae*	*cinquant*
sixty	*sessanta*	*soixante*
seventy	*settanta*	*soixante-dix*
eighty	*ottanta*	*quatre-vingts*
ninety	*novanta*	*quatre-vingt-dix*
one hundred	*cento*	*cent*

Days

English	Italian	French
today	*oggi*	*aujourd'hui*
tomorrow	*domani*	*demain*
yesterday	*ieri*	*hier*

English	Italian	French
Monday	*lunedì*	*lundi*
Tuesday	*martedì*	*mardi*
Wednesday	*mercoledì*	*mercredi*
Thursday	*giovedì*	*jeudi*
Friday	*venerdì*	*vendredi*
Saturday	*sabato*	*samedi*
Sunday	*domenica*	*dimanche*

Weather

English	Italian	French
weather forecast	*previsioni*	*météo*
snow	*neve*	*neige*
fog	*nebbia*	*brouillard*
storm (thundery)	*tempesta*	*orage (orageux)*
rain	*pioggia*	*pluie*
wind	*vento*	*vent*
sunny	*sole*	*ensoleillé*
cold	*freddo*	*froid*
hot	*caldo*	*chaud*
ice	*ghiaccio*	*glace*

Useful phrases

E: I would like to reserve ... dormitory places for tonight, please.
I: *Mi piacerebbe prenotare ... posti dormitorio stanotte, per favore.*
F: *Je voudrais réserver … lits pour cette nuit, s'il vous plaît.*

E: I would like to reserve … dormitory places for tomorrow night, please.
I: *Mi piacerebbe prenotare ... i dormitori domani sera, per favore.*
F: *Je voudrais réserver … lits pour demain soir, s'il vous plaît.*

E: I would like half board.
I: *Vorrei la mezza pensione.*
F: *Je voudrais la demi-pension, s'il vous plaît.*

E: I would like to buy … packed lunches please.
I: *Vorrei comprare ... pranzi al sacco, per favore.*
F: *Je voudrais acheter … pique-niques, s'il vous plaît.*

E: We will arrive …
I: *Arriveremo …*
F: *Nous arriverons à ...*

Accidents and emergencies

E: I have had an accident at …
I: *Ho avuto un incidente a ...*
F: *J'ai eu un accident à …*

E: My GPS location is …
I: *La mia posizione GPS è ...*
F: *Ma position GPS est …*

E: We have … casualties
I: *Abbiamo ... vittime*
F: *Nous avons … blessés*

E: He/she has injured his/her leg/head/back/arm
I: *Lui/lei ha ferito il suo/lei gamba/testa/schiena/braccio*
F: *Il/Elle a blessé son/sa jambe/tête/dos/bras*

E: We need a helicopter.
I: *Abbiamo bisogno di un elicottero.*
F: *Nous avons besoin d'un hélicoptère.*

E: We need an ambulance.
I: *Abbiamo bisogno di un'ambulanza.*
F: *Nous avons besoin d'une ambulance.*

E: We need help.
I: *Abbiamo bisogno di aiuto.*
F: *Nous avons besoin d'aide.*

APPENDIX D

Kit list

A typical two-week kit list is as follows:

- **Rucksack:** a 30–40 litre capacity rucksack should be large enough to fit the essentials and a few luxuries. Good ventilation and pockets will be of value on the trail
- **Boots:** worn-in boots that are stiff enough to resist rocky paths but flexible enough to be comfortable for long days on the trail
- **Underwear:** 3–4 pairs
- **Socks:** 2–3 'sets' – thin liner socks and thicker walking socks
- **Zip-off trekking trousers:** one pair will probably suffice, and a pair of shorts
- **T shirts:** 2–3. Merino-wool-based clothing can easily manage one week without becoming smelly but is expensive; synthetics are less resilient but much cheaper
- **Midlayer:** two should suffice and will allow some level of layering for higher altitudes/cold days. A thin duvet jacket may be of value in a chilly hut
- **Waterproof outer layer:** including overtrousers
- Light **gloves** and warm **hat/Buff**
- **Sun hat** with substantial brim
- **Suncream:** factor 30 or higher is recommended as the sun can be very strong at altitude
- Good-quality **sunglasses:** a wraparound style or with side guards to keep out glare; the sun is much stronger at altitude
- **Trekking poles:** a personal choice but very useful for long ascents and descents
- **Sleep wear:** (or use the 'spare' top)
- **Sheet sleeping bag:** a silk one is very light and will last decades
- **Ear plugs:** essential for busy dormitories!
- **Wash kit** and **towel:** many refuges now have showers
- A good **book** or **reading device**
- Personal **medication**
- Small **headtorch** for the dormitory

To be a considerate member of the *rifugio* community a spare, clean top is recommended; some synthetic clothing can harbour odours, and sitting next to someone who has worn the same top for days on end can be somewhat unpleasant!

Group equipment

- A small **first aid kit**, including **blister kit**
- **Maps, compass, guidebook**
- **Phrasebook**
- **Camera** and **spare battery** (recharging facilities can be limited in refuges)
- **Phone** (save battery life by keeping offline during the day)
- A bothy bag or some form of **emergency shelter** or cover
- Some liquid or powder **soap** for handwashing clothes; a few large **safety pins** are useful for pinning washed clothes onto a rucksack to dry on the trail
- A small pair of **binoculars** can be very useful for spotting distant wildlife

LISTING OF CICERONE GUIDES

SCOTLAND

Backpacker's Britain: Northern Scotland
Ben Nevis and Glen Coe
Cycle Touring in Northern Scotland
Cycling in the Hebrides
Great Mountain Days in Scotland
Mountain Biking in Southern and Central Scotland
Mountain Biking in West and North West Scotland
Not the West Highland Way
Scotland
Scotland's Best Small Mountains
Scotland's Mountain Ridges
The Ayrshire and Arran Coastal Paths
The Border Country
The Borders Abbeys Way
The Cape Wrath Trail
The Great Glen Way
The Great Glen Way Map Booklet
The Hebridean Way
The Hebrides
The Isle of Mull
The Isle of Skye
The Skye Trail
The Southern Upland Way
The Speyside Way
The Speyside Way Map Booklet
The West Highland Way
Walking Highland Perthshire
Walking in Scotland's Far North
Walking in the Angus Glens
Walking in the Cairngorms
Walking in the Ochils, Campsie Fells and Lomond Hills
Walking in the Pentland Hills
Walking in the Southern Uplands
Walking in Torridon
Walking Loch Lomond and the Trossachs
Walking on Arran
Walking on Harris and Lewis
Walking on Jura, Islay and Colonsay
Walking on Rum and the Small Isles
Walking on the Orkney and Shetland Isles
Walking on Uist and Barra
Walking the Corbetts Vol 1 South of the Great Glen
Walking the Corbetts Vol 2 North of the Great Glen
Walking the Galloway Hills
Walking the Munros Vol 1 – Southern, Central and Western Highlands
Walking the Munros Vol 2 – Northern Highlands and the Cairngorms
West Highland Way Map Booklet
Winter Climbs Ben Nevis and Glen Coe
Winter Climbs in the Cairngorms

NORTHERN ENGLAND TRAILS

Hadrian's Wall Path
Hadrian's Wall Path Map Booklet
Pennine Way Map Booklet
The Coast to Coast Map Booklet
The Coast to Coast Walk
The Dales Way
The Dales Way Map Booklet
The Pennine Way

LAKE DISTRICT

Cycling in the Lake District
Great Mountain Days in the Lake District
Lake District Winter Climbs
Lake District: High Level and Fell Walks
Lake District: Low Level and Lake Walks
Mountain Biking in the Lake District
Outdoor Adventures with Children – Lake District
Scrambles in the Lake District – North
Scrambles in the Lake District – South
Short Walks in Lakeland Book 2: North Lakeland
The Cumbria Way
The Southern Fells
Tour of the Lake District
Trail and Fell Running in the Lake District
Walking the Lake District Fells – Langdale
Walking the Lake District Fells – Wasdale

NORTH WEST ENGLAND AND THE ISLE OF MAN

Cycling the Pennine Bridleway
Cycling the Way of the Roses
Isle of Man Coastal Path
The Lancashire Cycleway
The Lune Valley and Howgills
The Ribble Way
Walking in Cumbria's Eden Valley
Walking in Lancashire
Walking in the Forest of Bowland and Pendle
Walking on the Isle of Man
Walking on the West Pennine Moors
Walks in Ribble Country
Walks in Silverdale and Arnside

NORTH EAST ENGLAND, YORKSHIRE DALES AND PENNINES

Cycling in the Yorkshire Dales
Great Mountain Days in the Pennines
Mountain Biking in the Yorkshire Dales
South Pennine Walks
St Oswald's Way and St Cuthbert's Way
The Cleveland Way and the Yorkshire Wolds Way
The Cleveland Way Map Booklet
The North York Moors
The Reivers Way
The Teesdale Way
Trail and Fell Running in the Yorkshire Dales
Walking in County Durham
Walking in Northumberland
Walking in the North Pennines
Walking in the Yorkshire Dales: North and East
Walking in the Yorkshire Dales: South and West
Walks in the Yorkshire Dales

WALES AND WELSH BORDERS

Cycle Touring in Wales
Cycling Lon Las Cymru
Glyndwr's Way
Great Mountain Days in Snowdonia
Hillwalking in Shropshire
Hillwalking in Wales – Vol 1
Hillwalking in Wales – Vol 2
Mountain Walking in Snowdonia
Offa's Dyke Map Booklet
Offa's Dyke Path
Pembrokeshire Coast Path Map Booklet
Ridges of Snowdonia
Scrambles in Snowdonia
Snowdonia: Low-level and easy walks – North
The Cambrian Way
The Ceredigion and Snowdonia Coast Paths
The Pembrokeshire Coast Path
The Severn Way
The Snowdonia Way
The Wales Coast Path
The Wye Valley Walk
Walking in Carmarthenshire
Walking in Pembrokeshire
Walking in the Forest of Dean
Walking in the Wye Valley
Walking on the Brecon Beacons
Walking on the Gower
Walking the Shropshire Way

DERBYSHIRE, PEAK DISTRICT AND MIDLANDS

Cycling in the Peak District
Dark Peak Walks
Scrambles in the Dark Peak
Walking in Derbyshire
White Peak Walks: The Northern Dales
White Peak Walks: The Southern Dales

SOUTHERN ENGLAND

20 Classic Sportive Rides in

South East England
20 Classic Sportive Rides in South West England
Cycling in the Cotswolds
Mountain Biking on the North Downs
Mountain Biking on the South Downs
North Downs Way Map Booklet
South West Coast Path Map Booklet – Vol 1: Minehead to St Ives
South West Coast Path Map Booklet – Vol 2: St Ives to Plymouth
South West Coast Path Map Booklet – Vol 3: Plymouth to Poole
Suffolk Coast and Heath Walks
The Cotswold Way
The Cotswold Way Map Booklet
The Great Stones Way
The Kennet and Avon Canal
The Lea Valley Walk
The North Downs Way
The Peddars Way and Norfolk Coast Path
The Pilgrims' Way
The Ridgeway Map Booklet
The Ridgeway National Trail
The South Downs Way
The South Downs Way Map Booklet
The South West Coast Path
The Thames Path
The Thames Path Map Booklet
The Two Moors Way
Two Moors Way Map Booklet
Walking Hampshire's Test Way
Walking in Cornwall
Walking in Essex
Walking in Kent
Walking in London
Walking in Norfolk
Walking in Sussex
Walking in the Chilterns
Walking in the Cotswolds
Walking in the Isles of Scilly
Walking in the New Forest
Walking in the North Wessex Downs
Walking in the Thames Valley
Walking on Dartmoor
Walking on Guernsey
Walking on Jersey
Walking on the Isle of Wight
Walking the Jurassic Coast
Walks in the South Downs National Park

BRITISH ISLES CHALLENGES, COLLECTIONS AND ACTIVITIES

The Big Rounds
The Book of the Bivvy
The Book of the Bothy
The C2C Cycle Route
The End to End Cycle Route
The End to End Trail
The Mountains of England and Wales: Vol 1 Wales
The Mountains of England and Wales: Vol 2 England
The National Trails
The UK's County Tops
Three Peaks, Ten Tors

ALPS CROSS-BORDER ROUTES

100 Hut Walks in the Alps
Across the Eastern Alps: E5
Alpine Ski Mountaineering Vol 1 – Western Alps
Alpine Ski Mountaineering Vol 2 – Central and Eastern Alps
Chamonix to Zermatt
The Karnischer Hohenweg
The Tour of the Bernina
Tour of Mont Blanc
Tour of Monte Rosa
Tour of the Matterhorn
Trail Running – Chamonix and the Mont Blanc region
Trekking in the Alps
Trekking in the Silvretta and Ratikon Alps
Trekking Munich to Venice
Walking in the Alps

PYRENEES AND FRANCE/SPAIN CROSS-BORDER ROUTES

Shorter Treks in the Pyrenees
The GR10 Trail
The GR11 Trail
The Pyrenean Haute Route
The Pyrenees
Walks and Climbs in the Pyrenees

AUSTRIA

Innsbruck Mountain Adventures
The Adlerweg
Trekking in Austria's Hohe Tauern
Trekking in the Stubai Alps
Trekking in the Zillertal Alps
Walking in Austria

SWITZERLAND

Switzerland's Jura Crest Trail
The Swiss Alpine Pass Route – Via Alpina Route 1
The Swiss Alps
Tour of the Jungfrau Region
Walking in the Bernese Oberland
Walking in the Engadine – Switzerland
Walking in the Valais

FRANCE

Chamonix Mountain Adventures
Cycle Touring in France
Cycling London to Paris
Cycling the Canal de la Garonne
Cycling the Canal du Midi
Écrins National Park
Mont Blanc Walks
Mountain Adventures in the Maurienne
The GR20 Corsica
The GR5 Trail
The GR5 Trail – Vosges and Jura
The Grand Traverse of the Massif Central
The Loire Cycle Route
The Moselle Cycle Route
The River Rhone Cycle Route
The Robert Louis Stevenson Trail
The Way of St James – Le Puy to the Pyrenees
Tour of the Oisans: The GR54
Tour of the Queyras
Vanoise Ski Touring
Via Ferratas of the French Alps
Walking in Corsica
Walking in Provence – East
Walking in Provence – West
Walking in the Auvergne
Walking in the Brianconnais
Walking in the Cevennes
Walking in the Dordogne
Walking in the Haute Savoie: North
Walking in the Haute Savoie: South
Walks in the Cathar Region

GERMANY

Hiking and Cycling in the Black Forest
The Danube Cycleway Vol 1
The Rhine Cycle Route
The Westweg
Walking in the Bavarian Alps

ICELAND AND GREENLAND

Trekking in Greenland – The Arctic Circle Trail
Walking and Trekking in Iceland

IRELAND

The Wild Atlantic Way and Western Ireland

ITALY

Italy's Sibillini National Park
Shorter Walks in the Dolomites
Ski Touring and Snowshoeing in the Dolomites
The Way of St Francis
Through the Italian Alps
Trekking in the Apennines
Trekking in the Dolomites
Via Ferratas of the Italian Dolomites Vol 1
Via Ferratas of the Italian Dolomites: Vol 2
Walking and Trekking in the Gran Paradiso
Walking in Abruzzo
Walking in Italy's Cinque Terre
Walking in Italy's Stelvio National Park
Walking in Sardinia
Walking in Sicily
Walking in the Dolomites

Walking in Tuscany
Walking in Umbria
Walking Lake Como and Maggiore
Walking Lake Garda and Iseo
Walking on the Amalfi Coast
Walks and Treks in the Maritime Alps

BELGIUM AND LUXEMBOURG

The GR5 Trail – Benelux and Lorraine
Walking in the Ardennes

SCANDINAVIA: NORWAY, SWEDEN, FINLAND

Trekking the Kungsleden
Walking in Norway

POLAND, SLOVAKIA, ROMANIA, HUNGARY AND BULGARIA

The Danube Cycleway Vol 2
The High Tatras
The Mountains of Romania
Walking in Bulgaria's National Parks
Walking in Hungary

SLOVENIA, CROATIA, SERBIA, MONTENEGRO, ALBANIA AND KOSOVO

Mountain Biking in Slovenia
The Islands of Croatia
The Julian Alps of Slovenia
The Mountains of Montenegro
The Peaks of the Balkans Trail
The Slovene Mountain Trail
Walking in Slovenia: The Karavanke
Walks and Treks in Croatia

SPAIN

Camino de Santiago – Camino Frances
Coastal Walks in Andalucia
Cycle Touring in Spain
Cycling the Camino de Santiago
Mountain Walking in Mallorca
Mountain Walking in Southern Catalunya
Spain's Sendero Historico: The GR1
The Andalucian Coast to Coast Walk
The Camino del Norte and Camino Primitivo
The Camino Ingles and Ruta do Mar
The Mountains of Nerja
The Mountains of Ronda and Grazalema
The Northern Caminos
The Sierras of Extremadura
Trekking in Mallorca
Trekking in the Canary Islands
Walking and Trekking in the Sierra Nevada
Walking in Andalucia
Walking in Menorca
Walking in the Cordillera Cantabrica
Walking on Gran Canaria
Walking on La Gomera and El Hierro
Walking on La Palma
Walking on Lanzarote and Fuerteventura
Walking on Tenerife
Walking on the Costa Blanca
Walking the Camino dos Faros

PORTUGAL

Portugal's Rota Vicentina
The Camino Portugues
Walking in Portugal
Walking in the Algarve
Walking on Madeira
Walking on the Azores

GREECE

The High Mountains of Crete
Trekking in Greece
Walking and Trekking in Zagori
Walking and Trekking on Corfu

CYPRUS

Walking in Cyprus

MALTA

Walking on Malta

INTERNATIONAL CHALLENGES, COLLECTIONS AND ACTIVITIES

Canyoning in the Alps
Europe's High Points
The Via Francigena Canterbury to Rome – Part 2

MOROCCO

Mountaineering in the Moroccan High Atlas
The High Atlas
Walks and Scrambles in the Moroccan Anti-Atlas

TANZANIA

Kilimanjaro

SOUTH AFRICA

Walking in the Drakensberg

TAJIKISTAN

Trekking in Tajikistan

JAPAN

Hiking and Trekking in the Japan Alps and Mount Fuji
Japan's Kumano Kodo Pilgrimage

JORDAN

Jordan – Walks, Treks, Caves, Climbs and Canyons
Treks and Climbs in Wadi Rum, Jordan

NEPAL

Annapurna
Everest: A Trekker's Guide
Trekking in the Himalaya

BHUTAN

Trekking in Bhutan

INDIA

Trekking in Ladakh

CHINA

The Mount Kailash Trek

NORTH AMERICA: USA AND CANADA

The John Muir Trail
The Pacific Crest Trail

SOUTH AMERICA: ARGENTINA, CHILE AND PERU

Aconcagua and the Southern Andes
Hiking and Biking Peru's Inca Trails
Torres del Paine

TECHNIQUES

Fastpacking
Geocaching in the UK
Lightweight Camping
Map and Compass
Outdoor Photography
Polar Exploration
Rock Climbing
Sport Climbing
The Mountain Hut Book

MINI GUIDES

Alpine Flowers
Avalanche!
Navigation
Pocket First Aid and Wilderness Medicine
Snow

MOUNTAIN LITERATURE

8000 metres
A Walk in the Clouds
Abode of the Gods
Fifty Years of Adventure
The Pennine Way – the Path, the People, the Journey
Unjustifiable Risk?

For full information on all our guides, books and eBooks, visit our website:
www.cicerone.co.uk

Explore the world with Cicerone

walking • trekking • mountaineering • climbing • mountain biking • cycling • via ferratas • scrambling • trail running • skills and techniques

For over 50 years, Cicerone have built up an outstanding collection of nearly 400 guides, inspiring all sorts of amazing experiences.

www.cicerone.co.uk – where adventures begin

- Our **website** is a treasure-trove for every outdoor adventurer. You can buy books or read inspiring articles and trip reports, get technical advice, check for updates, and view videos, photographs and mapping for routes and treks.

- **Register this book** or any other Cicerone guide in your member's library on our website and you can choose to automatically access updates and GPX files for your books, if available.

- Our **fortnightly newsletters** will update you on new publications and articles and keep you informed of other news and events. You can also follow us on Facebook, Twitter and Instagram.

We hope you have enjoyed using this guidebook. If you have any comments you would like to share, please contact us using the form on our website or via email, so that we can provide the best experience for future customers.

CICERONE

Juniper House, Murley Moss Business Village, Oxenholme Road, Kendal LA9 7RL

info@cicerone.co.uk cicerone.co.uk